HOW TO THRIVE
AS A
TEACHER
LEADER

JOHN G. GABRIEL

ASSOCIATION FOR SUPERVISION AND CURRICULUM DEVELOPMENT
ALEXANDRIA, VIRGINIA USA

ASCD®

Association for Supervision and Curriculum Development
1703 N. Beauregard St. • Alexandria, VA 22311-1714 USA
Phone: 800-933-2723 or 703-578-9600 • Fax: 703-575-5400
Web site: www.ascd.org • E-mail: member@ascd.org
Author guidelines: www.ascd.org/write

Gene R. Carter, *Executive Director*; Nancy Modrak, *Director of Publishing*; Julie Houtz, *Director of Book Editing & Production*; Genny Ostertag, *Project Manager*; Georgia McDonald, *Senior Graphic Designer*; Cindy Stock, *Typesetter*; Tracey A. Franklin, *Production Manager*

ASCD Member Book, No. FY05-04 (January 2005, PC). ASCD Member Books mail to Premium (P), Comprehensive (C), and Regular (R) members on this schedule: Jan., PC; Feb., P; Apr., PCR; May, P; July, PC; Aug., P; Sept., PCR; Nov., PC; Dec., P.

Paperback ISBN: 1-4166-0031-0 • ASCD product #104150 • List Price: $27.95
($21.95 ASCD member price, direct from ASCD only)

e-books ($27.95): retail PDF ISBN 1-4166-0185-6 • netLibrary ISBN 1-4166-0183-X • ebrary ISBN 1-4166-0184-8

Quantity discounts for this book: 10–49 copies, 10%; 50+ copies, 15%; for 500 or more copies, call 800-933-2723, ext. 5634, or 703-575-5634.

Library of Congress Cataloging-in-Publication Data

Gabriel, John G., 1973-
    How to thrive as a teacher leader / John G. Gabriel.
        p. cm.
    Includes bibliographical references and index.
    ISBN 1-4166-0031-0 (alk. paper)
    1. Teacher participation in administration—United States. 2. Educational leadership—United States. 3. Departmental chairmen (High school)—United States. I. Title.

    LB2806.45.G33 2005
    371.1'06–dc22

                                                    2004021622

12 11 10 09 08 07 06 05   12 11 10 9 8 7 6 5 4 3 2 1

To my parents
talented teachers in their own right

To the core E-Unit
an elite teaching machine

If you continue to do
what you have always done,
you will continue to get
what you have always gotten.

—Unknown

HOW TO THRIVE AS A TEACHER LEADER

Preface

As much as current educational literature points to the need for teacher leadership, there is scant realistic material written by teacher leaders explaining *how* to be an effective teacher leader. Such was the problem that I encountered when I was brought in as chair of the English Department at Falls Church High School in Fairfax County, Virginia, in 2001.

Falls Church High School, an extremely diverse school both ethnically and economically, had a passing rate of only 73 percent on the English Standards of Learning (SOL) test, one of Virginia's high-stakes tests that students must demonstrate proficiency on in order to graduate. With no formal leadership experience, I was expected to right the ship and steer it toward goals that seemed unattainable. At the time, the school faced a host of problems: a three-year downward trend in high-stakes scores, high turnover, low morale, apathy, student language deficiencies, and a high rate of free and reduced lunches, which is often indicative of underperforming schools.

These obstacles were imposing, but more so was the fact that I could find very little literature to guide me. I desperately searched for publications that would explain how to be an effective department chair, but my efforts were fruitless. There was a glut of literature about being an administrator, about being a teacher, but very few books dealt with one of the most slippery and challenging positions in a school building: the teacher leader.

Department heads usually lack formal training, and most are ill prepared for the position and its multifaceted demands: "Neither 'learning on the job' nor 'doing as their predecessors did' constitutes adequate training for effective job performance or for the preparation needed to perform their leadership responsibilities" (Weller, 2001, p. 80).

My situation was frustrating indeed, considering the pressure to improve test scores. So how to turn around a department in the face of barrier tests in a school renowned for underachievement? Hence, the impetus for this book.

At the end of my first year as chair, the department had improved to an 83 percent passing rate. By the following year, we were enjoying some of the highest SOL scores in Fairfax County, with a passing rate of 94 percent. Slightly more than one-third of our students were passing in the advanced range, statistics that put us on a par with the "better" English departments in the county.

So rather than presenting a text bogged down in research (although there is some to frame the issues), I thought it best to offer material grounded in actual experience and success, with practical suggestions—things that are sometimes lacking in educational discourse. Although this book is primarily geared toward teacher leaders or those aspiring to leadership roles, it includes tips and techniques that most every school employee could benefit from having in his or her educational toolbox.

But who exactly is a teacher leader? What constitutes effective teacher leadership? Given the current educational climate created by high-stakes testing and the challenge of finding ways to reach all children, these questions deserve particular attention. In addressing them, I categorize the charge of the teacher leader into four broad areas:

- Influencing school culture,
- Building and maintaining a successful team,
- Equipping other potential teacher leaders, and
- Enhancing or improving student achievement.

In order to be successful in these areas, a teacher leader must be a skillful communicator who can neutralize resistance, which will invariably and unfortunately arise from fellow teachers and even from administrators. At the same time, teacher leaders must find ways to create a positive climate and sense of community. A negative environment—one that lacks direction, unity, cohesiveness, motivation, shared ownership, and professionalism—can permeate teams and infect entire schools, which has a trickle-down effect on student achievement, standardized test scores, and morale. Therefore, dynamic teacher leadership is needed: leadership that can transform schools from houses of detention to houses of attention—for both student and teacher.

References

Weller, L. D., Jr. (2001). Department heads: The most underutilized leadership position. *NASSP Bulletin, 85*(625), 73–81.

Acknowledgments

There are many people to whom I am thankful for a variety of reasons.

First and foremost are my parents and family for their understanding during the writing process, their help, their advice, and their love, all of which I hope I have not taken for granted because I do realize how special they are and how blessed I am. Similarly, I am grateful to my friends for their interest, patience, and understanding over the past year and a half.

Thank you to Ron Scire and Antonia Valez of Lodi schools for starting my career; special thanks to my Stafford family, especially the following people: Greg Feducia for being my cooperating teacher; Bob White for bringing me to NSHS; Anne McGee for being such a supportive chair; Marian Parker for picking up where Anne left off; Karen and Kirk Darrough for treating me as one of their own children; Kevin Maine for many an intelligent conversation; Dewey Reynolds for working with me to improve education; Don Siegmund for helping set me up for success during my first year of advanced placement; Henry Johnson for encouraging me to apply to Fairfax; Julie and Jim Stemple and Judy Norton for their support; Maura Payne and Vanessa Sekinger for being such inspirations while we were at NSHS; and the rest of the NSHS faculty I learned from.

I am deeply indebted to Vera Blake, one of the most incredibly talented leaders I have ever known, for giving me the opportunity to come to Falls Church High School, for her patience and influence, and for putting me in contact with ASCD. Similarly, I am grateful to Paul Farmer for being a risk-taker, for providing me with numerous learning opportunities, for his guidance, instruction, and help, and for his willingness to be interviewed; Bob Graumann for our talks; and David Eschelman, whom I wish I could have worked with more. I would also like to thank the current FCHS administration, especially Daniel Ebeling and Janice Lloyd for their support during my tenure as chair.

There are many teachers I need to thank: Kristin Campbell Sheetz, whom I enjoyed watching grow as a teacher, for being one of the first people to embrace me, for giving me my nickname, for taking on a leadership role, and for her Reading Accountability Sheet; the exceptional Karen Wright Mackall for being so instrumental in effecting change, for being my anchor, my conscience, my voice of reason, and for the 11th grade curriculum map and tutoring schedule; Kim Torpey for making the right decision, for being one of the most extraordinarily dedicated and talented educators, and for her "Keeping It Together" handout; Lauren Young Kelly, who is more gifted than she will ever know and has the potential of being one of the stronger educational leaders of our generation, for her use of minutes and for helping proof the Test Prep Tip Sheet; the ever-understanding Medina Jones and the compassionate Ronna Traylor for their undying support; Anne Pegram for playing an integral role that can be thankless and unnoticed at times; Sue Halton for being such a classy person and a vital part of reform; Kelly Hoover for her diligence; Beth Harris for easing my transition during my first year; and the rest of the English Department at FCHS.

I am appreciative of the FCHS Instructional Council for allowing me the opportunity to work and grow with them; Jorge Gonzalez for his ESOL questions; Jim and Louise Hannon and Curran Roller for their math questions; Magda Cabrero for her kindness and foreign language questions; Heather Cole for helping me develop social studies questions; and the often underrecognized faculty of FCHS and anyone there I might have forgotten to include.

I would be remiss if I did not mention the following people as well: Lisa Green for her student teacher schedule; Mary Moriarty for taking me under her wing during my first year; Sandy Gutierrez for agreeing to be my mentor; Don Humbertson for having the patience to put up with a first-year department chair; Heather Bousman and Debbie Miller for educating me about special education; David Brazer for his insightful advice and our meetings; Jill and Bill Tucker for being the first ones to listen to my idea for a book; Susie Ellis for reading the first sample chapter, for being such a caring and supportive leader, and for having such strong shoulders to lean on; and Diana Welty Guerrero for her science questions, input, and encouragement, but especially for being such a selfless friend.

I would also like to thank Fairfax County Public Schools for the chance to begin my formal leadership career, and all the students I have had the privilege of teaching and learning from over the years.

Without you, none of this would have been possible.

1

Organizational Leadership

Nurturing Leadership
in Your School

For nearly a century, schools have functioned in the autocratic style of the line-staff model: principals are managers and teachers are their employees, often voiceless and powerless to influence their superiors' quest to improve student achievement. But with the growing emphasis on high-stakes testing and the advent of No Child Left Behind, many school leaders are seeking more effective organizational behavior by drawing on the leadership potential of all stakeholders, especially teachers.

Schools making this change are creating and expanding teachers' roles as leaders. For principals, this trend is a shift from "relying on the power of the system" to "seeking to empower others"—or, more specifically, a shift from "seeking to be in control" to "letting go of control and building a community of relationships that tends to be self-organizing" (Caine & Caine, 2000, p. 8). Lending support to the need for transformation, Buchen (2000) argues that "the only leadership that will make a difference is that of teachers. They alone are positioned where all the fulcrums are for change. They alone know what the day-to-day problems are and what it takes to solve them. They, not the principals, should be the ones to hire new teachers. They know what is needed."

A task force report from the School Leadership for the 21st Century Initiative (2001) echoes these sentiments. It states: "Mischaracterized though they often are as incompetent know-nothings, teachers are, paradoxically, also widely viewed as . . . indispensable but unappreciated leaders in the truest meaning of the word. . . . It would be difficult to find a more authentic but unacknowledged example of leadership in modern life" (p. 1). The report claims that teachers are essential to reform and that they possess a body of knowledge yet to be exploited.

Teachers can be dynamic forces fully capable of effecting change.

But we already knew that. That's common sense.

We educators also knew that the role ripest for this kind of metamorphosis is that of the department chair in high schools or the team leader in elementary and middle schools.

Department chairs and team leaders walk a fine line: they are neither teacher nor administrator. They nurture colleagues and teach alongside them, but they also must retain allegiance to their administrators. They lack line authority. Considering how essential teacher leaders are to improving achievement, this is perhaps the most curious aspect of their roles. They are constantly reminded, by both administrators and teachers, of all they cannot do—regardless of their potential for positive change, which is often greater than that of all other leaders in a school because of their broad sphere of influence.

Teacher leaders possess a semblance of authority but no formal power—only the illusion of power. For example, a department chair cannot complete teacher evaluations. She cannot place a memo or letter in someone's personnel file, nor can she dismiss a teacher. As a result, she must find other ways to motivate, mobilize, and lead teachers. She must rely on intrinsic leadership abilities, knowledge of group dynamics, influence, respect, and leadership by example to boost the productivity of her department.

In myopic schools, the role of department chair is limited to that of a paper pusher. These schools view the teacher leader as someone who will complete the master schedule, order supplies, maintain inventory, and pass along administrative directives to the department. These schools either don't know how else to capitalize on the strengths of their teacher leaders or are uncomfortable doing so. True, these traditional responsibilities are critical to maintaining the wellness of a school, but in terms of improving the health of an organization, forward-thinking schools have moved beyond this.

In schools where transformational leadership is present, administrators recognize that the leadership of a department chair or team leader can make a significant difference to the climate and culture of the school. They are not threatened by a teacher's influence or exercise of leadership, nor by giving up some control. These administrators strive to encourage and cultivate leadership and "make better use of the unique strengths and contributions [that] department heads can bring to school management and improvement" (Weller, 2001, p. 80). At these schools, teacher leaders act as coaches and mentors, observe classrooms so that instruction can be refined and best practices implemented, and attempt to realize a vision or to "reculture" the environment. With the pressure of high-stakes testing and the need to meet state and federal benchmarks, administrators rely on these leaders to improve achievement and even defer to them in certain instances.

Roles for Teacher Leaders

Although the traditional teacher leader is still important in a school, other leadership positions can have as much influence in ensuring student achievement. These roles offer teachers a greater voice in shaping programs, supporting the mission, and guiding a team toward its goal, which will ultimately help the students and the school achieve.

Not all leadership positions are formal in nature. Every school has teacher leaders who do not serve—and may never have served—as official leaders, which is one of the most unique components of teacher leadership. In any kind of organization, informal leaders command a great deal of respect; they have much say and sway in determining a team's climate or the chances of a proposal's adoption, and they are often sought after for advice.

Similarly, not all leadership roles are fixed—meaning assigned, specific positions. Someone might act as a mentor one week and then assume the role of innovator with a unique proposal the following week. These fluid and spontaneous roles are just as essential as the leader to the success of the team. Ideally, these people are the supporters whom the leader can trust and turn to for help in a variety of matters.

It is also expected that leadership roles will change, shift, and evolve over time. If someone was a team leader for the past five years, it does not guarantee him that role for a sixth year. Leadership roles should not be determined by seniority. Therefore, if standardized results are marginal or a teacher's leadership is questionable, a change is warranted. Don't be afraid to make changes; change, along with its potential for struggle and conflict, is often an essential ingredient of success.

Leaders are both teachers and learners.

If you are a department chair or team leader, you probably have already realized how difficult it is to accomplish everything that your job entails. Effective teacher leaders are usually given more responsibility, whether they want it or not, so you need to learn how not to overburden your teachers and how to say no (and that there is nothing wrong in doing so) to avoid burnout. Although the following leadership positions can enhance teachers' professional self-worth, these roles are equally significant to you: delegating (not avoiding) responsibility is critical if you hope to succeed as a leader.

Moreover, these roles can be vehicles for grooming future leaders. Aside from becoming a department chair, counselor, or administrator, a teacher has very little opportunity for career advancement within a school building. Not only can the leadership possibilities below benefit a school or a program, they can also spark interest in pursuing a position at the central office or collegiate level, where teachers can have an even greater influence on education.

Grade Level/Subject Area Leader

The grade level leader coordinates specific organizational needs (whether the 5th grade will take its annual class trip to Philadelphia, what supplies to order, and so on), and he runs meetings that address concerns and strategies regarding specific students.

This leadership position is often further broken down by content area or instructional concerns. Through horizontal alignment, the subject area specialist coordinates curriculum across the grade level, providing instructional leadership and support to teachers of a common subject. For instance, the subject leader might call a meeting to discuss why some 6th graders are having more success than others in comprehending photosynthesis, and which strategies have been effective in conveying the concept.

Monitoring the instruction and assessments of the teachers on the grade level is paramount since every student in each subject area is expected to possess the same set of skills and body of knowledge at the end of the year. These leaders initiate curriculum mapping and scrutinize the assessments used. Analyzing data also plays a large role in improving student achievement, so leaders should be aware of the most recent data about the team and its progress toward certain benchmarks. Finally, these leaders create staff development opportunities for their teams, because they best know the challenges that the teams face.

Vertical Leader

This role is similar to the above, except that the leader is in charge of seeing that curriculum is aligned up and down the grade levels. For example, the 6th grade vertical team leader ensures that students have acquired the knowledge and skills in their previous math classes that they need for success at the benchmark level. If not, leaders find ways to tighten the instruction and the curriculum. They also promote collaboration and share pertinent content literature.

Backup Leader

Train future leaders by rotating teachers as the backup to your position. Invest time to sit down with them and explain the nature of your job, or to discuss situations that arise during the course of your day. You might have them proofread one of your e-mail messages so they can learn about the issues you deal with (plus, it is always a good idea to have an extra set of eyes look over something you wrote).

Let them join you in interviews. Afterward, meet with them immediately to explain your line of questioning or to see what characteristics of the applicant they picked up on. Send them in your place to meetings where they will learn how time-consuming, and at times frustrating, a leadership position can be and how to cope with that. Have them assume your responsibilities when you are absent.

Basically, let them experience your experience, similar to an informal internship where they can get an overview of your position and its nuances. While you are equipping them with essential skills and knowledge, you may be creating your successor for when you move on. Even if you don't leave in the near future, your back-up will have been trained to take a leadership position elsewhere. As one of my administrators used to preach, begin the cycle anew and help reform education from within.

Mentor

This person takes on the responsibility of coaching and advising novice teachers and teachers who are new to the school system. With more and more novice teachers leaving the field within the first few years of teaching, the mentor is not only concerned with instructional and organizational needs; he also lends emotional and moral support to alleviate the stress that the job creates.

A mentor need not always be the strongest instructional leader, but he should have a solid grounding in best practices and his content area. He should be able to suggest ideas and strategies to assist in classroom instruction. And he must be astute enough to read people (that is, he must be perceptive and have a high emotional intelligence). Because of the importance of retaining teachers, new employees should be carefully placed and matched with mentors, either by a lead mentor, who oversees mentors in the entire building, or by the team or department leader. (See Resource 1.)

Peer Coach

Not a new concept, peer coaching has received much attention in recent years and is embraced and advanced in some school districts. A peer coach is similar to a mentor except that with this pair, both teachers—not necessarily novices—function as mentor and as protégé. In this relationship, the word "peer" is key. Because peer denotes equality, these teachers' classroom visits are non-threatening. They are not evaluative and prescriptive; they are diagnostic and constructive, allowing teachers to experiment and take risks without fear of judgment.

After each has observed the other in class, peer coaches discuss observed instructional behaviors, actions, and practices, which can include giving feedback on plans, lessons, instruction, classroom presence, and classroom management. There is a safe environment among these volunteers that enables them to converse in a candid manner and learn from each other. This ultimately benefits the teachers' growth, the team's growth, and the students' growth.

Note-Taker/Recorder

It is imperative to keep a record of every meeting because we tend to have selective memories, especially when we are passionate about an issue. An accurate record of what was discussed and what was decided can be helpful in case of future disagreement, as well as in bringing people who missed the meeting up to speed.

Minutes should document who was present, who was absent, and who was late. Working from an agenda, the note-taker keeps a record of issues and questions raised and the resulting dialogue, outcomes, and resolutions. In circumstances where there may be rancor over what the minutes reflect, it might be prudent to have two people record them and compare notes to ensure their accuracy.

Although it might be interpreted that the note-taker is in cahoots with you if she sits next to you, proximity can be helpful. It enables her to look over your shoulder at your own notes in case she misses something and to stay on top of every issue. It is also a good idea to keep the minutes in a central place so all teachers, regardless of what team they are serving on, have access to them.

Parliamentarian/Timekeeper

This person alleviates the team leader's responsibilities by keeping the group on task with the agenda. After a stressful day of work, it is natural for a meeting to degenerate into a complaint session or, in worse cases, a complete digression into the social lives of the group's members. This leader keeps the group plowing ahead and reminds members when they are nearing the cutoff or have exceeded the time limit for a topic. Meetings should be productive, and the main reason they often are not is that someone has been allowed to derail the group and pursue his own topics of discussion while everyone waits for someone else to intervene.

Presenter

Too often schools are obsessed with spending money to send teachers to conferences outside the system when the answers, knowledge, and resources are right there within their own walls. Both weak and strong school systems tend to underuse the extraordinary wealth of talent they possess.

Target one of your teacher's strengths and ask him to give a presentation. Or ask someone, or a team, to read a professional article and report back to the group on it. This role is by no means fixed. For example, the team leader can begin by selecting someone to present. Then the role should rotate through the team, perhaps in a "popcorn" fashion (often used during reading activities), where the last person to present picks the next person to present. This kind of staff development should be the focus for most of your team meetings.

Conference Attendee

After you have exhausted your team's resources, try to send your teachers to seminars, depending on your budget. They should also attend local, state, and national conferences. However, this should not be a free vacation. The attendee should clearly understand that she is responsible for bringing information back to the team at the next meeting. This sharing can lead to further meeting topics and action research.

Speaker/Writer

Have your teachers identify something that they do extremely well and encourage them to polish, organize, and market it by submitting proposals to present at conferences. Or encourage them to share their experiences and successes by writing articles for various educational journals. These are great opportunities for them to grow professionally and to network—and it brings your school good publicity. Moreover, if they impress someone with their presentation or article, then that could turn into a speaking engagement—a chance to make a few extra dollars with little additional preparation. As one colleague explained, a strong presentation is like an annuity because it keeps on paying.

School Plan Chair

Contrary to how it is viewed and used (or not used) in some schools, the school plan is a vital, fluid document that should guide your team toward improving student achievement. The role of school plan chair usually does not rotate because consistency and continuity are extremely important. The school plan chair has an integral position in coordinating and guiding the school toward achieving its vision.

People should not feel penalized for holding this position in spite of the work it might entail. If your school functions in a collegial and cooperative manner, a team leader or department chair will not have to bear the brunt of this responsibility. The school plan chair should be charismatic, compassionate, and organized. She will be working with all the teachers in the building; a group effort is needed to create or enhance this document.

Faculty Representative

Some school systems have faculty councils where teacher leaders bring team, department, and faculty issues to the administration. If teachers are concerned that a tardy policy is not being enforced, for example, then the faculty representative would bring this issue to the council. Other school systems have a council where teachers can bring issues directly to the superintendent. If teachers are concerned about the number of inservice days that the county is mandating, this would be the forum to bring such a concern. And, finally, some schools have instructional councils that teachers sit on, where leaders discuss issues pertaining to classroom and buildingwide instruction.

A faculty representative seeks out the questions, concerns, and issues of his colleagues and brings them, verbatim when possible, to a more powerful body. He could set up a drop-box in the building or, with the aid of the building's technology specialist, establish an e-mail account that would protect the anonymity of teachers posting or sending messages. This leader brings back minutes to the team or school so people know what has been decided and can confirm that their concerns have been accurately represented.

A union representative is a similar position. A strong teacher advocate, the union rep listens to faculty concerns and works closely with the administration and external bodies. This leader, who in many ways is a watchdog, protects and ensures teacher interests, advises teachers who believe their rights have been infringed, and, in some states, plays a role in negotiating contracts.

Host Teacher

A host teacher is someone who is willing to sponsor a practicum student or a student teacher from the local college or university. Finding the right match is crucial; you want the visiting student to have the best and most realistic experience possible. Some host teachers might view this role as a vacation because someone else will be responsible for teaching their classes. It should be stressed that hosting a student teacher involves much time and can even be quite burdensome, especially if the person is not as well prepared as he should be.

This leader models exemplary instructional practices, techniques, and strategies for the student teacher to observe during his stay. After the student teacher has observed the host teacher's classes for a couple of weeks, the bulk of the teaching load is turned over to him. The host teacher assists with unit and lesson planning and helps him create assessments. Although it would seem that the host teacher has fewer responsibilities because she is teaching fewer classes, she has the responsibility of coaching and mentoring the aspiring teacher. She observes classes, provides timely and meaningful feedback and constructive criticism to her student teacher, and conferences with both him and the college supervisor regarding his progress.

If a team leader or department chair isn't the host teacher, he should meet with the student teacher to provide an overview of the program and its policies. Meeting again at the end of the student's stay to answer lingering questions will provide closure to the experience.

Instructional Audit Leader

Every public school must go through some kind of an accreditation cycle. This leader serves on the school's accreditation committee by gathering evidence to demonstrate that the school is meeting certain standards; he meets with the visiting committee, and then reports its recommendations to the school or relevant team and assists in making any necessary changes. A variation of this role is for a teacher to serve on the committee that visits schools on the cycle. In doing so, the leader can learn more about the functioning of the total school and its programs and can bring back information about successful programs and ideas.

Search Committee Panelist

In schools where administrative applicants must interview with a panel—a team usually consisting of the principal or her designee, teachers, and, in some cases, even parents and students—a teacher might enjoy having a hand in finding the best fit for the school and community by sitting on such a panel. Although he might not have a voice in creating the panel questions, he can, with the principal's permission, canvass the school to determine the characteristics and qualities the faculty is looking for in their new administrator. If he has the principal's trust, he might even be the one to organize and coordinate the panel; he could review résumés or tap other teachers to serve with him on the team.

Community Leader

All teachers should be involved in their communities not just because of the obvious reasons but also because of the political ramifications. At a time when budgets are slashed because community members do not have children attending the local school and are loath to pass a tax increase, and when a significant portion of the public believes that teachers work only "9:00 to 3:00 and have summers free," PR work is needed to demonstrate the many services that a school provides and the good things that occur there.

Teachers can reach out to the surrounding community by volunteering to teach courses in their areas of specialty, by attending community functions to show their support, or by attending community meetings to keep abreast of concerns. Attending PTSA meetings or serving as a liaison between the PTSA and the faculty is another way to build connections.

Teachers can also exhibit leadership by actively engaging the community. A leader I know initiated a "community and texts" program, a kind of book club where every student, parent, and community member was invited to read the same book and meet at the school for book talks. This leader had incredible success in uniting property owners and businesses and showcasing the innovative things the school was doing.

Other kinds of community outreach can be targeted solely at parents. I hosted two events, one on the SAT and one on our AP program, so parents could become better informed. Securing guest speakers, sending letters home in multiple languages, and using the PTSA to promote the events drew some of the largest audiences the school had seen and did wonders in involving parents in their children's education.

Student Activities Coordinator

Often an administrator is the one to oversee the placement of sponsors and coaches to the groups needing sponsorship. But a teacher might be able to forge a tighter bond between students and organization sponsors by finding the best match. A good match could have a direct influence on student achievement because, as some literature suggests, extracurriculars and achievement are related. In addition to overseeing student groups, this leader might encourage teachers to become sponsors or encourage groups to plan joint events.

Technology Leader

This person does not initially need to be the technology guru of the team. She should have an interest in technology, but she can be trained in this area. The leader coordinates the team's technological needs and serves as a troubleshooter when glitches arise. If your building has a technology committee, she serves as a liaison to that group and assists in making buildingwide decisions concerning technology.

Web Page Curator

This position is best suited for a technophile. Many teachers love technology and crave the opportunity to demonstrate their knowledge of it—and will jump at the chance to use it. Tap these feelings and abilities by making someone responsible for creating or monitoring a department or team Web page. This can be a vital resource for parents and students in addition to being a great PR vehicle. This person might create links to other helpful Web sites, post bios of your teachers, write an online newsletter, or work on anything else that would be beneficial to the learning community.

Supplies Coordinator

A supplies coordinator may not be necessary on all grade levels or in all subject areas. For example, a high school history department may be concerned only with books and traditional supplies, but a 7th grade science team might need someone to coordinate the use, inventory, and ordering of lab equipment and supplies. This leader's responsibility is to determine what the team needs and ensure it has the materials for success.

Leadership Qualities

Although the options for leadership are varied, there are a number of qualities that leaders have in common. Many of these characteristics are seen in effective teachers, which might be why people gravitate toward them and why they seek leadership positions. Look for the following traits in the teachers in your department and in your school, and steer your potential teacher leaders toward growth opportunities.

Principled

One of the problems with U.S. politics today is that few representatives are willing to take a stand and fight for what they truly believe in. It's not surprising that people are apathetic and voter turnout is consistently low. People want someone to believe in, someone who will "fight the good fight" and risk the consequences of doing so, and teachers are no different.

It would seem that tenured teachers have little to lose because they have job security, but repercussions can take the form of having their schedules changed, being forced to "float" between rooms, not receiving administrative support, or being unable to advance in their careers. A teacher who weighs these risks and still wants his voice heard over the din is a leader whom people want to work with and to follow. These teachers are student centered and not motivated by stipends or how being a leader makes them feel.

A principled person is also trustworthy. Earning the trust of colleagues is no small feat, and maintaining confidentiality can be difficult sometimes. Those who confide in you expect you to keep information to yourself, and if you do, you can be rewarded in a variety of ways.

Honest and Ethical

By choice or not, people will generally follow their leaders. If a leader is honest and ethical, however, he will be respected, which is more important. An elementary school team leader was asked not to tell one of his teachers that she would be inheriting a very disruptive student midway through the marking period. If he withheld this information and was later asked if he had previous knowledge of it, he would either have to lie, which he was uncomfortable doing, or admit the truth, which he believed would diminish his leadership.

The day he learned of the news, he decided it was best to tell the teacher after school what was going to happen the next day. Consequently, the teacher respected him for being forthright and treating her as a professional. He was able to prevent her emotional outburst, which would have occurred the following day when the disruptive student walked into her classroom—and which would have affected the teacher, her students, the leader, the guidance department, and the administration. And his leadership was strengthened as a result.

Organized

A disorganized teacher leader would be hard-pressed to handle all her responsibilities inside and outside of the classroom while holding a leadership position. Organized, though, does not mean that every paper is tucked neatly away in a manila folder or that a workstation is spotless. Being organized means having some kind of system in place, however foreign it may appear to others, to stay focused and on track, which facilitates being able to handle the myriad responsibilities necessary for teaching and leading.

Perceptive

Nowadays, too few people listen carefully to what others are saying, and too many ignore facial expressions, gestures, and other clues. Being sensitive to people's needs and concerns is crucial. It is essential to be able to discern when your team is overwhelmed, when a meeting ceases to be productive, and when your teachers need assistance or direction but are reluctant to ask for it.

Sensing what people need and when they need it is a key leadership quality. Successful leaders are able to read people. They mentally note people's reactions and remember certain situations, and they are able to connect the dots along the way. They perceive differences between what people say and what they do. They are observant, as they note the school politics, identify potential threats, and adjust accordingly so that their actions are not damaging. Trusting their instincts is another way that these leaders are effective: they know when to go with their gut.

Empathetic and Supportive

People are more inclined to follow someone who understands what they are going through. It is not good enough for a leader to imagine what it is like to have a class of 35 freshmen; she needs to have had such a large group herself. This is why administrators who had only a brief tenure in the classroom, or who never taught, have a tough time leading: they are unable to convince their constituency that they have "been there, done that." A lack of direct experience makes it difficult for them to provide viable and valuable suggestions to teachers, or for teachers to trust and act on recommendations they receive.

An empathetic and supportive leader assists others emotionally, socially, and instructionally, and forges connections with them. Without being judgmental, she finds ways to help people recognize and learn from their mistakes. She is not intent on punishing people but instead on helping them.

Altruistic

Much as a mother feeds her children first when there is not enough to go around, those who put the needs of others ahead of their own have a solid understanding of what true leadership entails. The sacrifice may involve waiting until everyone else receives supplies or taking on an unappealing task. Leaders sacrifice their planning periods, their free time, and sometimes even their personal lives for the benefit of others. A leader understands that the health of the family depends on letting others eat before she does.

Accessible

The concept of having an "open-door policy" has lost almost all its cachet. Some profess it but don't practice it, whereas some preach it but make others feel awkward for taking advantage of it. We obviously should be accessible during contract hours. But because the nature of the job demands that we often take our work home, we should be accessible after hours as well.

An administrator made himself accessible to me by giving me both his home phone number and his cell phone number, and when I called, he never made me feel that I was intruding on his time. He understood that for us to be successful, these kinds of sacrifices were necessary. In turn, all my teachers have my contact information. When a new hire needed to reach me, he was astonished when a colleague gave him my cell phone number, exclaiming, "You mean he doesn't mind if you call him during the weekend?"

Of course, you need to set limits. I know a department chair who would receive phone calls from one of her teachers several times a week simply to talk about his day. This chair was going beyond being accessible; she was unable to set and communicate boundaries.

Resourceful

Obstacles do not slow down a good leader; they are opportunities for him to flex his problem-solving muscles. People are inspired to work with a leader who can circumvent roadblocks, devise creative solutions, and use the network. For example, a resourceful teacher does not accept a shortage of funds as the bottom line; he knows whose pockets to pick or finds people to subsidize the team's needs.

Fair

Being professional means putting aside personal prejudices for the good of the students. A fair leader hears all voices, does not play favorites (although she may have them), and is not self-serving. Treating everyone fairly is more important than treating everyone equally, and a fair leader is an impartial leader. She does not allow friendships or rivalries to impede the group's progress, especially when moving toward improved achievement. She understands that she walks a fine line, expresses that to her teachers, and practices fairness toward all whenever possible.

Accepting

Accepting people for who and what they are shows leadership. Although placing blame may make a leader feel more secure, it is better for the group if he accepts people's flaws and shortcomings and learns how to work with them (or around them). Also, rather than passing the buck, accepting the blame for a problem demonstrates responsibility. Teachers respect and want to work with leaders who are willing to be accountable, a rare quality indeed in our current age of abdication of responsibility.

Vulnerable

Leaders who own up to mistakes or share their errors with their colleagues, with an explanation of what they learned from the experience, are valued. Leaders who admit mistakes show a willingness to grow. They are perceived as human, not as unapproachable academics in an ivory tower or arrogant know-it-alls. Not afraid to admit when they do not know an answer, they are willing to learn and ask others for the answers. And humility can be refreshingly disarming.

Forward-Thinking

Some people have a knack for anticipating what might happen next. Whether it is predicting the outcome of a meeting or a situation or analyzing political and educational trends, the ability to plan for what may be coming down the pike is a talent that not many possess. Successful athletes demonstrate this on a regular basis by just seeming to know what is needed or where they are needed. Successful teacher leaders are no different. Conducting a parametric analysis (where education is, where it has been, and where it is headed) can put a team on the cutting edge. Leaders can save their group time and growing pains by suggesting change and giving choices rather than mandates, which are always less palatable.

Futurists are often risk-takers. The teacher in a previous scenario who had the dilemma of whether or not to inform a colleague about a decision is a risk-taker of sorts. He was not foolhardy; he did not rush into the situation but weighed the risks and the consequences and took action. As General George S. Patton once remarked, taking calculated risks is quite different from being rash. Examples of risks include piloting a new idea or strategy or supporting someone who is willing to do so. Similarly, these people seize the initiative instead of waiting for others to act. They recognize the far-reaching effects of a good idea and get the ball rolling.

Global

Seeing the bigger picture is a skill that facilitates problem solving. A teacher leader is not always able to understand why decisions are made and how they affect the entire organizational structure, but she does comprehend the ramifications on her team. She is able to see beyond her classroom to at least her hallway. She doesn't deal in scraps; she deals in what is best for all students and teachers.

Decisive and Incisive

Leadership demands an action-oriented, decisive person: those leaders who get things done are the most appreciated. They take the initiative and make things happen. Penetrating to the heart of an issue shows a keen and quick mind—and it can save time. In a profession where time is limited and people spend an inordinate amount of time discussing, debating, and deliberating issues, respect belongs to the person who, without making a rushed decision, can consider all angles and cut to the chase.

Intelligent

Intelligence as a key quality may sound obvious, but a leader I know was not respected because he lacked depth in his content knowledge. Once teachers realized this, they ran academic circles around him to hide what was really going on in their classrooms, and students used this to their advantage to help them get what they wanted.

Similarly, teachers resent leaders who simply give an answer because they are expected to have one. Students can sense when adults fake their way through an explanation, but adults can be more perceptive and unforgiving. Even though it seems that anti-intellectualism is rampant in our society, educators value intelligence and crave an intelligent leader.

The Leadership Choice

You already possess a powerful strategy for improving achievement: nurturing teacher leadership. Most people want to feel that they are part of something significant, that what they do matters, and that they are contributing members to a common goal that affects achievement. Teacher leadership meets this need because it creates a greater sense of ownership, buy-in, and community.

Although administrators hold influential positions in guiding a school toward its goals, it is the teacher leader's interpretation, support, and implementation of decisions—his and the administration's—that move an organization forward. He simultaneously deals with a myriad of obstacles and runs interference so that an avalanche of issues does not deluge the main office.

If a teacher leader is effective, he will rarely need to disturb an administrator, and what administrator would not appreciate more time to devote to her responsibilities? In fact, by taking on more responsibility or solving problems creatively, he can build rapport with her. The teacher leader, in turn, will be better supported by his administrator, which will ultimately increase his effectiveness. Moreover, because of high-stakes testing, administrators are spending more time out of the building at workshops, meetings, and training sessions or promoting the school, so the need for teacher leadership has never been more obvious. Identify those teachers in your department who are integral to its success and train them as teacher leaders.

There will be those who rise to the challenge and those who attempt to knock them down. Leadership breeds envy, and we teachers can be very petty people sometimes. What is baffling is that we're not envious of other teacher leaders because of what their positions bring. Most often, no tangible rewards are associated with teacher leadership. Many department chairs and mentors receive some kind of financial compensation, but dedicated leaders do not take on these roles for remuneration (and it usually is nominal in relation to the hours they spend).

Most teachers accept leadership as a reward in itself: they derive a sense of self-worth from having their voices heard, developing vision, or serving their students and colleagues. Desirable as this satisfaction is, it should hardly evoke envy or (at worst) maliciousness. But it can. I'm not here to explain human nature but to remind you that these kinds of feelings and behaviors exist.

To mollify those who are discontented, you or an administrator might be tempted to grant them leadership positions. This tactic might work in some cases. Perhaps putting such people in the spotlight will unleash their latent leadership abilities or force them to step up to the plate. This is not always the case, however, and such a decision can backfire with horrendous consequences. Remember that the business of educating children is not Little League baseball: everyone does not get a chance to swing the bat. A score is kept, and there are winners and losers. To give everyone a chance to play, regardless of ability, is damaging to students and can be even more damaging to the game.

Our student athletes realize this. Students are not selected to start on the varsity team simply because they are seniors. They know that it takes more than a desire and a commitment to win: their abilities determine their roles. To use another analogy, a high-profile legal case is not given to a lawyer simply because it is his turn in the firm to have one. That would not be serving a defendant's interests. Lawyers receive such cases because they earn them. The same should hold true for your teachers. If adolescents and other professionals can understand this concept, you need to believe that your teachers will understand it also. If a teacher who lacks leadership qualities and abilities feels it is unfair that she does not have a leadership position, find another way to make her feel valued.

References

Buchen, I. H. (2000, May 31). The myth of school leadership. *Education Week, 19*(38), 1–3.

Burns, J. M. (1978). *Leadership*. New York: HarperCollins.

Caine, G., & Caine, R. N. (2000). The learning community as a foundation for developing teacher leaders. *NASSP Bulletin, 84*(616), 7–14.

School Leadership for the 21st Century Initiative. (2001, April). *Leadership for student learning: Redefining the teacher as leader*. Washington, DC: Institute for Educational Leadership.

Weller, L. D., Jr. (2001). Department heads: The most underutilized leadership position. *NASSP Bulletin, 85*(625), 73–81.

2

Strategic Leadership

Assembling Your Team

With the dearth of quality teachers available because of teacher turnover and the profession's meager pay, building a successful team can take an extraordinary amount of time and effort. It will often require conducting numerous interviews to find the right match for your school and for your team, but the investment will save time in the future and will ultimately return dividends to you in the form of student achievement. And finding the best match for your team will have a direct and immediate positive effect on students.

Unfortunately, teacher leaders are rarely asked to interview applicants for teaching positions. Instead, assistant principals are the ones who conduct interviews. Principals typically delegate this job to assistant principals because they are viewed as *the* instructional experts: good teaching is good teaching, regardless of the discipline, and administrators are supposed to know it when they see it. An assistant principal doesn't supervise only the subject area that she once taught, if she taught at all; she is responsible for three or four (in some cases, more) different disciplines, and regardless of the subject matter, she should be able to identify what makes those teachers effective.

An assistant principal might have a strong grasp on cooperative learning, differentiation, or some other pedagogical concept, but is a former physical education teacher capable of asking a candidate about the efficacy of whole language versus phonics in a reading class? Is a former math teacher able to discuss the writing process in an English class? Is a former art teacher able to ask about problem solving versus drill-and-practice in an algebra class? Not likely.

Perhaps some have been in administration so long that they can interview an applicant as competently as an expert in the subject area, or maybe some are such voracious readers that they can deftly handle themselves when talking with candidates from foreign disciplines. But do they constitute the majority of administrators who interview prospective teachers? Probably not. And what about the novice administrator? Surely he has had limited experience in working with other disciplines.

Yet this is how schools function. Consider the following scenario:

Katie, a social studies department chair of six years, informs a table full of her teachers at lunch during the first day of inservice week that their assistant principal hired a new teacher to replace someone who resigned. Katie is immediately deluged by a torrent of questions about the new hire. Male or female? Young or old? What's she like? Does she sound knowledgeable? Is she from the area or out of state? Is she a good match? Has she taught honors before?

All Katie can say is that Sandy Howe is a young woman who graduated from a nearby university—nothing else, because she was not asked to sit in on the interview. She explains that she would be meeting Sandy for the first time with the rest of the department the next day. One teacher betrays his surprise when he exclaims, "Really!" The others either look knowingly at one another or roll their eyes. One teacher privately tells Katie after lunch that he took classes with the applicant in college. He elaborates that he never felt extremely confident in her abilities and has much anecdotal evidence to support his perceptions.

A month into the school year, it is clear that Sandy has good control over her classes and a well-managed classroom. Students are familiar with its routines, pay attention for the most part, and have not been referred for any infractions. Some students even like her. But others confess in private that "Ms. Howe doesn't know what she is talking about." Students have begun to realize what the teachers learned during inservice week: Sandy is very competent in the mechanics of her classroom—management and organization—but her knowledge of her subject area, and how to best communicate it, is severely lacking. Students have noticed her inability to answer medium to difficult questions, gaps in her knowledge, and often incorrect and inaccurate explanations of material.

One day when Sandy is absent, a couple of teachers admit at lunch that similar complaints have made their way to them from parents. Katie nods her head and admits that she is aware of the situation. She has heard the same whispers in the building and was summoned to a meeting earlier that morning by her administrator.

In this scenario, based on an actual situation, it became the responsibility of the chair to find a way to bring the teacher up to speed with the rest of the team. Even with several hours of observations, meetings, and the like, she was still unsuccessful. After expending much time and energy over the next few months, she helped her administrator build a case to deny reappointment.

But what if the situation were slightly different—what if the chair were aggravated by her exclusion from the hiring process and insulted that she was asked to help clean up the mess? She could manipulate the situation by fomenting teachers' frustration in order to rally them against the administration, especially if she had an axe to grind.

Adhering to this time-honored model of the administrator holding the interviewing reins does not benefit students; in fact, it often creates more problems in the long run and can be dangerous. Aside from being a strain and drain on resources, it weakens the chair's leadership and her teachers' respect for her. It can cause teachers to resent their administrator by thinking he doesn't trust their judgment or their leader's abilities. If the new hire is perceived as a weak link in the department, it perpetuates the stereotype of an administrator being ineffectual or being too far removed from the classroom. Not to mention what happens once parents are thrown into the mix. This is hardly an efficient or effective way to build a department.

Candidates are less likely to throw out jargon or content-based circumlocutions if the teacher leader, the content expert, is present in an interview. He is the one who possesses a thorough understanding of not only the subject matter but also its nuances and the philosophical debates inherent in it. He is the one who is closest to the action. He is the one who has a firmer grasp on a department's strengths, weaknesses, and needs. He is the one who will end up working the closest with the new teacher.

Compare this to certain sports organizations. The front office and ownership make suggestions, and many of them can be fruitful, but it is the coaches—who are not as distanced as management because they are on the field with the players day in and day out and best understand what must be done—who make the logical personnel decisions. All too often, however, teacher leaders are left on the sidelines. Their exclusion from the interviewing process is even more perplexing if they are viewed as instructional leaders and are asked to coach new hires or provide assistance to struggling teachers.

Teacher leaders can be integral agents of change when involved in interviewing.

And what does the new hire in the previous scenario think about her chair when she meets her for the first time? Whether the administrator intended to or not, the message he sends the new teacher is that he does not respect or value the chair, so neither should she. When her chair needs to talk with her about instructional issues, she reacts negatively to observations, comments, and suggestions or ignores them altogether.

To avoid the fallout of these potential land mines, a former administrator always insisted on involving his chairs in interviewing. Not only did he view his chairs as instructional leaders and experts in their areas, but he also believed that it was essential for incoming teachers to be loyal to their chairs. If such a bond is created, a teacher is more likely to work harder for his chair, to work with him instead of against him, and to maybe become a more conscientious department member. This administrator was correct in his assumption about loyalty: several of my teachers worry more about letting me down than letting down an administrator and, as a result, try harder to be better teachers. Perhaps more important, *I* worry more than they do about letting *them* down because I was the one who brought them onboard.

If you do not currently interview your own candidates, ask your administrator to join her in an interview to observe her questioning techniques (and, by doing so, you'll open the door for a second opinion to be in the room; it's only natural for your administrator to ask what you thought of the candidate). If training is necessary for you to take on this duty, seek it out. Then work your way up to conducting interviews where you take the lead. You might also ask if you can accompany your supervisor to job fairs or on recruitment trips. Touch base or debrief with your administrator after these events. Once it is evident that the two of you are on the same page regarding candidates and she trusts your judgment, she might allow you to take on the bulk of this responsibility—freeing her up to devote more time to other concerns.

If you continue to find yourself excluded from this area of leadership, then simply ask, "How will we [the two of you, the department, the school, or the students] benefit from that?" Instead of asking why you aren't involved, you're asking your administrator to explain the positive outcomes of your exclusion in assembling your team. That is not an easy question to answer.

Expanding the Applicant Pool

Where do you find strong applicants? What should you look for in an applicant? What should you ask (and not ask) in an interview? The efficacy of your leadership depends primarily on the answers to these questions, so you obviously want to find ways to bring in the best teachers possible.

Practicum Students and Student Teachers

If a local college or university in your area sends students to your district for field experience, capitalize on this by agreeing to host practicum students. Although hosting them can often be time-consuming, this is not only a chance to assist future teachers in their careers, which can be rewarding in and of itself, but also an opportunity to bolster your applicant pool (or, conversely, reduce your applicant pool). By developing a student teacher–friendly environment, you can create and foster a pipeline between a college and your school. If your practicum students have a positive experience in your building, they are more likely to want a job there and promote your department and school among their peers who will be seeking placements and jobs in the future.

Basically, hosting a student teacher gives you the opportunity to groom a future teacher, one who is already familiar with your school, its population, and its policies. This can be invaluable because it can save much time sifting through résumés, sitting through interviews, and mentoring. The student teacher will already have made connections with students, parents, and staff, which can make her first year easier.

When hosting practicum students, go above and beyond the norm by assuming that they will eventually be a part of your department. It is helpful to give them a packet that contains a building map, bell schedule, list of emergency exits for fire drills, and your department's philosophy, curriculum, and program of studies. Meet with them ahead of time to determine what their goals are, and similarly meet with them at the end of their stay to debrief and discuss what they have observed. Expose them to a variety of teaching styles and a variety of classes, which can dispel their preconceived notions about teaching, student abilities, student work, and education in general. (See Resources 2 and 3.)

Meet with your host teachers so that they are aware of expectations, and stress the value of sharing materials. Some of the best resources aspiring teachers receive will be from their practicum experiences, not from their actual courses, so provide them with a resource file and give them materials even for classes they are not observing, because they might end up teaching them in the future. Additionally, make sure that your teachers treat their student teachers as colleagues, as equals, as members of the department.

In terms of with whom you should place these aspiring teachers, remember that people are not given leadership positions based on seniority. Match the practicum students with those teachers who are willing to work with them but also with those who can provide them with the most positive experience. This could be their first experience in a school setting. Imagine how you would have felt if you had been placed with someone who simply punched a time card or who was a yellow-note teacher (which is how some teachers refer to those who have been using the same notes and resources for the past 30 years—all their papers are yellow from age because they have not changed a single practice). Instead, give your student teachers something to look forward to: a dynamic teacher who cares about kids and is open to assisting novice teachers.

Provide student teachers with a rich, realistic experience.

If you decide to match your practicum students with several different teachers, it might cross your mind to include a weak teacher in the mix so that they can learn what not to do. Even though this can serve a worthwhile purpose, proceed with caution. You certainly don't want your teachers to believe that this is why they were chosen to host someone. It also creates a poor image of the school (essentially advertising that there are bad teachers in your department), which is not the impression you'd want to make on a prospective employee.

At the end of a student teacher's stay, have him complete an evaluation or survey to help you determine how to better serve future college students, which will ultimately help your department (Resource 4). You might even offer to be a guest speaker for your student teacher's education class or volunteer to participate in a panel discussion; doing so will make an impression on prospective teachers and give your school greater publicity.

Professional Memberships and Conferences

As it stands anyway, professional memberships and organizations are fantastic resources, but in this case they are even more useful for the purpose of networking. If you are able to forge positive relationships with members, they might tell you about someone who is looking for a job, considering transferring, or moving into the area. If you can provide this kind of information for them, they might be more inclined to return the favor. The same applies to conferences. If you are able to establish contacts at local, state, and national conferences, you might be able to get the jump on a candidate before another school.

Churches, Bazaars, and Community Events

One principal advocated posting or distributing write-ups of the department, school, and vacant position at various community events to broaden the applicant pool. This will certainly attract a large number of people who don't have any training, let alone experience, the kind of people who will say, "I've always been told I would be a good teacher" or "I thought I would give it a try."

Although the chances are slim that you will find a teacher by advertising this way, you might trigger a chain of events that will bring you an applicant. For example, an uncle attending a chili cook-off might come across your flyer and pass it along to his niece who is graduating college in a month and starting her job search. Another advantage to this method is that you are reaching out to the community and attempting to involve it. Although this strategy might not yield results, the possibilities are endless and the potential is strong.

School Web Sites

If your school has a Web page, promote your department through it. An interesting and informative Web page can attract a candidate to your building and tip the scales in your favor. Create an eye-catching home page (or a separate section for applicants) that will impress prospective teachers who, in this technological age, often visit Web sites before applying to a school.

In addition to wanting contact information, candidates will also want to get a feel for your department or team, whether it is a good fit for them. Provide your department's philosophy, mission statement, program overview, and test results (even if the scores are not up to par—you don't want to appear to be hiding anything). You might choose to explain your bell schedule, how your school day is organized, what a teaching load generally consists of, and other information that candidates inquire about during an interview. Because you will be competing with other schools in your district or neighboring school systems, do as much as possible to set yourself apart: persuade an applicant that he wants to work in your building.

What Are You Looking For?

Obviously, there are numerous desirable characteristics to look for in a prospective teacher, including many of the leadership qualities discussed in Chapter 1. Some interviewers might place greater value on one quality over another, which is natural because of people's varying views on education and on their subject areas. But there are certain characteristics that you should definitely consider in an applicant, which fall under the areas of academic, personal, interpersonal, and leadership intelligence. As a teacher leader, you will eventually discover that candidates possessing the following qualities tend to be more effective and can make your job easier.

High GPA

In years past, many interviewers did not place much weight on GPA when evaluating an applicant. I would like to say it was because educators have certain perceptions about what grades tell them or can tell them, but I don't believe that was entirely the case; this was where the pendulum had swung at the time. With the advent of No Child Left Behind, the pendulum has swung in the other direction: one's content knowledge is of greater import as teachers are considered "highly qualified" or "not qualified." Although a high GPA can signify subject matter knowledge, a candidate's GPA in education classes can suggest knowledge of instruction and of how students learn. Also look for a candidate who would like to continue his education in the future, because this shows a willingness and desire to grow.

Open-Mindedness

What a high GPA does not necessarily indicate is one's openness to continued growth and intellectual inquiry. You want a candidate who is open to learning new ideas on her own as well as to hearing about new ideas from colleagues, which are often two very different things. Such a person will research new ideas and strategies and stay up-to-date with educational literature. Determine how "current" your candidate is in her content area by asking current events questions about relevant issues being discussed in the news, in educational journals and newsletters, at professional conferences, and the like.

An open-minded person welcomes a colleague's input or offer of help in the form of ideas, lessons, or activities. She is willing to try new things, and maybe repeat things if they did not work the first time around. Her initial reaction does not kill an idea ("We already tried that and it didn't work then"), but instead she nurtures a suggestion if it can potentially blossom into a solution. She also demonstrates a willingness to work collaboratively with colleagues and can accept and grow from constructive criticism.

Work Ethic

Teachers are usually only required to work seven and a half hours a day, but we are all familiar with the reality of the job's demands. Therefore, you need someone who subscribes to this reality as well. You cannot ask candidates in an interview if they would be willing to work after the contract day has ended, but you can identify these teachers because they demonstrate that they care about kids and will be there for them in all kinds of ways even when not required. You can also determine this by seeing how willing they are to sponsor activities not attached to stipends.

Even though assessing a candidate's work ethic is sometimes difficult, certain characteristics often signify a strong work ethic. For example, you want someone who is serious and energetic, which is slightly different from being enthusiastic. Although you do want an enthusiastic teacher, enthusiasm is merely excitement and interest; that doesn't always translate into vigor and rigor, which is power, effort, and the drive to accomplish things. A serious person cares about what he does, takes pride in his work, and sees the value in what he does. The bottom line is that you want, as a colleague once commented, someone who has job integrity and is not just committed to keeping a job.

Confidence

It might sound odd, but knowing how to be confident is a kind of intelligence. Even those who possess extraordinary abilities don't always believe in themselves. You want someone who does, or at least someone who can with little prodding; you don't want someone who is constantly coming to you with questions or second-guessing himself, or who is perpetually insecure. He must know how to promote himself without seeming cocky, because, as the cliché goes, there is a fine line between confidence and arrogance. A confident teacher has strong convictions and believes in himself. He not only is up for the challenge, but he can and he will meet that challenge. He is not blinded by hubris; he understands that he still has room to grow, does not have all the answers, and will be the first to ask for and heed advice.

Confidence inspires and bolsters confidence in others.

Confidence is important to a new teacher and to a teacher new to a building, because classroom management will often hinge upon it. Even though the following comparison is ostensibly repulsive, there is much truth to it: students are like dogs in that they can smell fear and will turn on someone when they sense it. Students need to respect their teacher, and respect is not automatically given. It is earned. To complete this analogy, students generally want to respect their teacher the same way a new puppy wants to respect its owner. Students crave structure, routine, and discipline. They want to follow their leader just as a dog wants to follow the pack leader. But one would not beat a puppy to housebreak it; likewise, discipline in a classroom should never be extreme.

An arrogant teacher, on the other hand, believes that only his views and ideas are valid; he does not believe in another's ideas, and even when opinions or philosophies coincide, he maintains that his are different lest he have to admit equality with his peers. He annoys people when he is right, refuses to believe he could be wrong, irritates colleagues both personally and professionally, and feigns gratitude but is indignant when given advice. A teacher's arrogance will turn students off to learning and hinder any bonding with them. Such a personality will never allow for student input or feedback on the state of the learning environment.

Intuition

If you stress collaboration on your team and expect your teachers to form meaningful connections with their students, then you want someone who is able to relate to people. This person knows how to read people's emotions; she is patient, skilled in diplomacy, and a good negotiator. She understands what it is like to be a student in today's day and age, but she also recognizes the need for accountability and personal responsibility. She holds high expectations, tempering them with generosity and leniency when appropriate. She has a rapport with a wide range of students. Recognizing and realizing why people—both students and teachers—behave the way they do is crucial for preventing conflict, enhancing learning, facilitating communication, and leading.

Leadership Potential

It is perfectly acceptable to hire people who don't necessarily have leadership experience or potential. Not everybody is a leader, can be a leader, or wants to be a leader. At the same time, you should hope to find candidates with leadership potential. You need these people for their ability to influence, their innovation and vision, their enhanced sense of responsibility, and their willingness to take initiative. Because people have professional and personal goals, they will not stay forever in your department; you need to consider who will replace whom, who is willing and eager to step up to the plate to push the team ahead. It's a good idea to ask candidates about their leadership goals and their leadership experience in and out of the classroom.

Interviewing an Applicant

Whether he is a teacher or an administrator, an effective educator usually trusts his instincts in almost every situation he faces daily. This is no different when it comes to interviewing. Even though many school divisions have scoring rubrics and sample responses to guide an interviewer in how to rate an applicant, his decision often comes down to what his instincts tell him. But it is nearly impossible to explain what your gut should tell you, could tell you, and will tell you. So there a few basic things to keep in mind when conducting interviews.

Preparing for the Interview

First, if you are in need of building trust and community on your team, meet with your teachers beforehand to see what kind of person they believe the team needs. Discuss the kinds of questions that should be asked and create sample responses and rubrics for them. General questions might include the following (and I hope the reasons for including them and the potential responses are obvious):

- What is your philosophy of education?
- How would you describe an effective classroom?
- What is your classroom management style?
- What routines do you have in your classroom?
- How do you structure a class on the block schedule?
- What kinds of activities could I expect to see in your classroom?
- Do you differentiate instruction? If so, how?
- For what reasons do you assess students?
- How do you assess them? How often?
- How do you remediate unsuccessful students?
- What are your feelings toward high-stakes testing?
- Does technology play a role in your classroom? If so, how?

- What activities are you willing to sponsor?
- What leadership positions have you held?
- Can you describe a time when your leadership brought about a positive outcome?
- What recent professional article had an influence on you?
- Are you fluent in any other languages?
- What sets you apart from other candidates I will be meeting with?

These questions work for all disciplines, but gearing them toward the content area will enhance them. And to better evaluate the applicant, you should definitely complement general questions with content-specific ones (Resource 5).

Questions that you can't ask typically include, but are not limited to, the following: age, marital status, origin or race, sexual orientation, and religious beliefs. You should consult your human resources department for more specific and current information.

When questioning your candidate, avoid asking leading questions. This happens when you have subconsciously embedded the answer in the question or made what you are looking for in an answer obvious. For example, consider the difference between "What alternative assessments do you use in your classroom?" and "How do you assess your students?" The first question has an answer and values hidden in it. You are expressing to your prospective teacher that he *should* use alternative assessments and that you value an array of assessments. The second question is more open-ended and does not lead the applicant to the answer. If you ask leading questions, you will discover that your interviewee is responding with what he *thinks* you want to hear.

Conducting the Interview

Remember that your applicants will be reading you as you will be reading them. After I made the recommendation to hire a young teacher, she confessed that she thought she had "bombed" the interview because she was unable to pick up on any positive signs from me. Although you do want an applicant to be comfortable, you don't want to tip your hand in any way. Even nodding your head in agreement or complimenting someone on a response can yield such a result. If the candidate detects what he should be saying, this does little good: it can lead to trouble later if he is hired.

You want an honest candidate, someone who has his own opinions, views, and philosophies and is not afraid to share them. This kind of candidate wants to find a place where he fits. If his philosophies don't mesh with yours, he ultimately won't be able to support the bigger picture.

There will be times when a candidate from out of state cannot interview in person and will request a phone interview. These situations are unavoidable, but don't let a phone interview be the only one you conduct. Although you can learn much about the candidate, the impersonal nature of this kind of interview prevents you from getting as best a feel for him as possible. Before recommending him for hire, insist that he come in for a traditional interview.

When conducting the actual interview, keep the following techniques in mind:

- **Tolerate silence.** Just because a candidate is quiet or takes a few moments to respond to a question, that does not necessarily mean that she does not have an answer or is slow on her feet. Interviewing can be a stressful process, so give your candidates some leniency in this regard.

- **Ask for concrete details.** The questions you ask should be pointed enough that you don't need to follow up on them. However, if a candidate is nervous, you might sense that he has an answer to your question but is unable to express it. As you would with your students, find a way to redirect without indicating what you are looking for in a response.

- **Avoid debate.** An interview is not an occasion for you to engage in philosophical debates. Even if you strongly disagree with something that an applicant says or believes in, there is no need to argue the point with her or convince her that you are correct. Simply not recommending her for hire is enough.

▪ **Don't interrupt.** Excited and enthusiastic as you might be by what your candidate has to say, never interrupt him. Doing so will reflect poorly on you and your leadership skills.

▪ **Maintain eye contact.** Show that you are interested in what she has to say or present by maintaining eye contact during the interview. Memorizing or being very familiar with your interview questions and their sequence can help you accomplish this. If you don't demonstrate strong eye contact, you might convey to your candidate that you are not interested in her or, worse yet, that you cannot be trusted.

▪ **Listen more, talk less.** As in most interpersonal situations, sometimes the less you say the better. Your task is to get your applicant to reveal as much as possible through probing and follow-up questions, so keep your talking to a minimum. If you take the candidate on a tour of the school or if he gets the job, then there will be plenty of time to discuss points that you found interesting.

▪ **Limit response time.** Some candidates, either through their exuberance or ignorance regarding the question, will talk for what seems like an endless amount of time. Because you might have scheduled back-to-back interviews and need to remain on schedule, develop ways to subtly curtail candidates' responses without making it appear that you are cutting them off.

Concluding the Interview

Place a reasonable time limit on your interviews. One colleague conducts marathon sessions that last nearly an hour and a half. Although this kind of interview is advantageous in that it can give you a better feel for the candidate, it has several drawbacks. The length can drain the interviewee, so she might not be as sharp as she could be, through no fault of her own. By extension, it can have the same effect on you, especially if you have several interviews scheduled in one day. And that is another consideration: you need to get through as many interviews as possible in a professional and timely manner. Limiting them to approximately 30 minutes gives you the opportunity to interview more candidates, which is important considering you still have your normal responsibilities of grading, planning, and helping your teachers.

Reserve the final 5 or 10 minutes for candidate questions and for an overview of your school. Be as honest as possible. Imagine what would happen if you blurred the truth or were not especially forthcoming: the candidate would eventually discover the truth when brought onboard. As a result, your reputation, integrity, and professionalism would be questioned and you would have a difficult time earning back that trust. After a candidate asks questions, tell her about your school and your program—the population, demographics, curriculum, teacher responsibilities, building or department history, and so on. If she interests you, promote the strengths of your team and your school and the benefits of working in your building, or take her on a brief tour of the school to showcase its highlights. You might direct her to your Web site or create a profile sheet of your school and department for her to refer to later as she weighs her options and offers from other schools.

- **Document everything.** When I began participating in interviews, an administrator stressed the value of having a system to document them—a system that would not only help me to identify the candidate in the future but also enable me to recall the person. You should document anything and everything related to a candidate. This administrator recommended housing all résumés and related materials in a loose-leaf binder for at least a year. Log the date you received the applicant's résumé, when you first made contact, when you subsequently spoke with him, and what transpired during your conversations. Recording details of the interview is obviously a good idea, but the administrator also suggested writing a brief, impartial description of the candidate ("Tall, bearded with glasses, originally from NY"). Make sure your notes remain confidential and objective. Finally, include in the binder copies of all pre- and post-interview e-mail and correspondence.

- **Check references.** Most administrators handle this responsibility. But if you are able to take it on, then do so, because you might ask questions that your supervisor did not think of. Start with the obvious questions about the time period the applicant was employed, what she taught, what activities she sponsored—basically follow up on what she has presented in her résumé. What you can ask a reference depends on various laws, but you should be able to ask about an aspirant's strengths and weaknesses. Get the reference to offer as much information as possible and to do most of the talking.

You should check at least two references, but consider whom you will call—will it be her college professor, administrator, principal, department chair, or cooperating teacher? As stated earlier, those closest to the action have the best idea of what is going on. For example, an assistant principal might have conducted only the minimum number of observations required for evaluation (sometimes less than two a year, if they were performed at all), and a professor might have known the applicant from only one class. But a department chair or host teacher could comment on what he observed on a daily basis, what consistently went on inside a classroom: he would be able to speak to the kind of teacher who would be joining your team. You should also think about whom the applicant did not list as a reference and why. Some interviewers often call those people first because omissions, like breaks in employment history, raise eyebrows. Investigate any discrepancies (why the applicant's assistant principal has a different take than her department chair, for instance). And as with everything else, be sure to document your reference checks.

Placing Your Hires

With such high turnover in education, it is essential that you take an active role in the development and nurturing of your new teachers. To safeguard them from leaving because they are overwhelmed by the job or disillusioned by it, provide them with resources for success. Even if they are comfortable with the subject matter or have developed strong lesson plans during their student teaching experience, you have more experience than they do. Share it. New teachers don't have the background you possess when it comes to handling students, parents, classroom management, or conflicts with other teachers.

That does not mean that your expertise or advice will always be welcomed with open arms. At the very least, novice teachers will want to make their own mistakes; at worst, they won't want input because they firmly believe that they already know all there is to know. To use a personal example, when I first started teaching, I knew everything. I truly believed it. My arrogance and obstinacy were due to my youth and inexperience; I thought I had encountered all that I needed to know during my field experience and student teaching. But just over a year later, I was able to see how little I knew and recognize how much I had grown. Such an experience is not unique. In talking with new teachers over the past few years, I have discovered they underwent similar transitions. Therefore, be tactful in how you handle assisting and developing your new teachers.

Mentoring and Monitoring New Teachers

Do everything possible to set up new hires for success. Create a new teacher packet that they can acquaint themselves with over the summer. This handbook can include pertinent articles and information about planning, instruction, assessment, and classroom management; handouts of graphic organizers; philosophies related to your content area; and anything else that might help. The packet you create should be manageable enough to easily navigate through and digest; it should augment a teacher's educational background and not serve as a crash course in teaching.

Pairing your new teachers with a mentor is another key stopgap in preventing turnover. New teachers are new to the complexities, intricacies, and headaches that the job presents. Even experienced teachers who are new to the school will have questions about how the building functions, at the very least. New hires need someone to help guide them through their first year, if not longer. Give them someone they can confide in, someone willing to aid them in their growth. If your building has a mentor program, advocate for the teacher who would be the best match in your department. If no program is available, you can always serve as the mentor or ask someone on your team to do so and find ways to support and reward her.

Give your teachers a solid foundation to ensure success.

One of the main stresses for a new teacher is keeping track of the many things she needs in each of her classes, so offer ways to help her stay organized and manage her responsibilities. The lead mentor in my building does this by giving her teachers an organizer to keep in their plan book, which helps them stay focused on what needs to be done for specific periods beyond lesson plans (Resource 6).

Although it might sound underhanded, keep tabs on what goes on in your new teachers' classrooms. A highly respected department chair, who had been recognized as a teacher of the year, used to monitor what her new teachers were doing by having them share rooms with her more trusted teachers. Sometimes she would check up on new teachers by speaking with students in the hall to see how things were going. I never felt as if she were spying on me, and she always had a fairly accurate idea of what was going on in my classes and when she needed to get involved.

Master Scheduling

Creating your department's master schedule will be one of the most taxing and frustrating responsibilities you take on as a leader.

The master schedule is a complex, ever-changing puzzle, and there is often no correct answer or multiple correct answers. Which classes need to be offered during which periods, which teachers need certain periods off because of other responsibilities, how other departments affect your schedule, and other variables can cause you to go through several drafts of your schedule before the opening of the school year.

Most teachers have little knowledge about what goes into creating the master schedule, which is why they are baffled upon returning in August to discover that they are no longer teaching what they had been assigned when they left in June. You certainly don't want to devote an entire meeting to explaining the process of master scheduling, but it is a good idea to briefly illustrate why the schedule can change or why it might be impossible for some teachers to have their dream schedule.

At March's department meeting, I distribute "wish lists" to my teachers to determine what they would like to teach the following year, and I try to honor at least one request per teacher (Resource 7). If a teacher's schedule changes drastically over the summer, contact him so he can adjust accordingly. Those leaders who don't do this ignore the reality that most teachers revise plans and refine other elements of their classrooms over the summer. Giving your teacher advance notice will allow him to get a much-needed head start if he will be inheriting an entirely new prep, and it demonstrates that you are a responsive and caring leader.

When determining a teacher's load, try your best to limit preps to two. Three preps can be manageable to a veteran teacher, but a new teacher could drown under that kind of responsibility. You also need to safeguard against teachers teaming with more than one special education teacher. This kind of load creates an abnormally heavy burden on both the core and the LD teachers because the odds increase that they won't have a common planning period. And, when possible, eliminate singletons. This occurs when a teacher has four classes of one grade level or subject and one class of something else. When a teacher has this kind of schedule, most of his focus is on the four similar classes; the singleton does not receive as much attention because he does not have as much invested in it. At times, that class might even be an afterthought.

Perhaps the overriding question is, Who should teach which classes? In addition to matching people to their strengths, there are some guidelines to follow as a general rule:

- **Don't give a teacher all honors or advanced placement classes.** Give teachers of advanced classes a balanced schedule so that they teach students of varying abilities. This helps keep teachers grounded and prevents others from accusing you, or the teacher, of favoritism.
- **Don't automatically give weaker teachers accelerated classes.** A colleague was in a situation where she was asked to give an ineffective teacher—one who was simply punching the time card until he retired—advanced classes because it was assumed that he would do less damage to those students. There is no easy answer to the predicament of what to do with such a teacher. But one thing you can count on is that the parents of those students are generally the most vocal, and they will be up in arms. Similarly, don't give accelerated classes to senior teachers just because they believe that it is their turn to have them.
- **Let people grow and develop in their classes.** Don't rotate someone out of a class because she has taught it for a couple of years. It can take three to five years for someone to get a comprehensive grasp on the subject matter (and perhaps even to tire of it). Therefore, don't be in a rush to move someone out of a class even if someone else wants to try it or believes it is her turn.
- **Preserve successful teams.** If you have a successful team consisting of a core teacher and an LD teacher, protect it at all costs from being split up. The unspoken reality is that, for a variety of reasons, too many teamed situations border on being dysfunctional. Tap these successful team teachers for leadership roles where they can share their

expertise and mentor and train other team teachers; showcase these effective teams and let them serve as models for other teams to observe.

There are other scheduling considerations besides which classes your teachers would or would not like to have. For example, if your school is on a traditional seven-period school day, you need to adjust your schedule so that your teachers don't go five periods before their first planning period or have two planning periods back-to-back. Similarly, if you teach on an alternating block schedule, you need to ensure that your teachers have a planning period each day. If you are unable to guarantee these things, it could have an adverse effect on morale and, by extension, on student achievement.

You are only as good a leader as your team is strong, which is why the hiring and placement of your teachers is of strategic importance. A strong leader can have his leadership diminished by a weak team; a weak leader can have his leadership enhanced by a strong team. Student achievement hinges upon good teaching, so your leadership should and will affect achievement. By advocating for your involvement in the interview process, you will have a greater chance to positively influence student achievement. You are *the* instructional leader or subject expert, and you will often know best what your team needs. So don't be silent when it comes to assembling your team. Ultimately, you are hurting students by remaining quiet.

3

Interpersonal Leadership

Communicating Your Leadership

The successful leader is an articulate leader. A dynamic speaker motivates people; a powerful writer persuades people. A weak speaker, but perhaps a competent leader, might never earn his colleagues' respect. Similarly, a leader's poor writing skills may distract people from his strengths. Just as we are judged, for better or for worse, by our appearance, we are also evaluated on our oral and written communication skills.

The leader who can articulate his vision and effectively communicate with colleagues has already won half the battle in demonstrating his leadership abilities and earning respect. His teachers are more likely to have confidence in him. Although you may not have the time to devote to becoming a better speaker or writer, you can pick up some easy techniques for becoming a more polished communicator and, as a result, for becoming more skillful in working with your teachers.

Written Communication

E-mail

Rapidly disappearing are the days of receiving mounds of paper in our in-boxes to inform us about meetings, events, and policies. But widely used as e-mail is, there are still those unaware of proper e-mail etiquette. For example, one colleague uses multiple font colors in her e-mail messages, one of which is red—a color we associate with anger. Because she also puts entire sentences in capitals, which signifies shouting, and in bolded type, which suggests emphasis but can sometimes indicate anger, teachers often misconstrue her e-mails: they take offense to something that might not have been intended to offend because her formatting choices create an antagonistic tone.

Another teacher justified his similar e-mails by commenting that "e-mail is meant to be informal communication." That may be the case in our social lives, but, quite simply, work-related e-mail is for professional purposes. Therefore, messages should be formal in nature, and your format should reflect that. Use a conservative style rather than ornate fonts to reflect your professionalism, to help ensure that you are taken seriously, and to make your e-mails easy to read.

Additionally, e-mail should be brief. A short e-mail does not necessarily make it a curt one: your diction will determine that. We may have much to communicate in an e-mail, but if it goes on for pages, the intended audience will lose interest. If you have much information to relay, e-mail a brief overview and request a meeting. Also, using bullets or some other kind of indentation to set off main points better organizes your text and makes it easier to follow.

Very rarely are we given opportunities to determine exactly what we want to say and how we want to say it, so proofread your e-mail and carefully choose your words. Don't rush to send an e-mail. Review what you have written by scrutinizing your word choice and sentence structure, because these elements help establish your tone. Ask yourself what tone is present, if it can be misconstrued, and if you would be comfortable if your e-mail was shared with someone else.

But do demonstrate that you are a responsive leader by replying to an e-mail, or at least acknowledging it, within 24 hours when possible. If a teacher e-mails you with a question or request, acknowledge receipt of the e-mail rather than waiting to respond once you have an answer. These kinds of delays cause confusion and frustration for teachers. They will either continue to e-mail you, thereby inadvertently clogging your in-box and creating more work for you, or they will simmer and complain to their colleagues that they are not being heard, which will weaken your leadership.

Memos

As Joe Friday used to say, "Just the facts, ma'am." Heed his advice. Because a memo is a more official form of communication, you should use objective language to record an incident or to pass along information. Your feelings have no place in a memo; never state that you were upset or disappointed by something the recipient has (or has not) done. Simply note what has transpired, or whether someone has met his obligations or neglected them.

Clear communication is essential to a team's success.

A memo should usually be briefer than an e-mail message, and the subject line should accurately reflect the content. If it is necessary for anyone other than the recipient to receive the information, include these people (often at the bottom of the page) with an "xc." (Many businesses have replaced "cc," carbon copy, with "xc," xerox copy, because carbon paper is nearly obsolete.) Teacher leaders do not have the power to place a memo in someone's file— only an administrator can do that—but that does not mean they shouldn't write memos. (See Resource 8.)

Letters

A good leader will make contact with her teachers over the summer. Administrators send letters to the faculty over the summer, and teacher leaders should follow this example. A welcome-back letter can be breezy, lighthearted, or straightforward, but it should introduce new team members, recap the successes of the year, and summarize what the new year will hold (Resource 9). And if someone on your team is taking on a new leadership position, why not welcome her aboard and show your professionalism by sending her a letter to congratulate her and detail her responsibilities? (See Resource 10.)

Style

How you write is as important as—if not more important than—what you write. Obviously, your writing should be free of typos and grammatical mistakes. When it is not, at best, your authority is diminished. At worst, when your writing is riddled with errors, people question your intelligence and lose their faith in your leadership. Clear, concise writing aside, there are certain tricks that make for more effective communication.

Consider these two sentences:

1. I wrote a referral because he cut class, was disrespectful, and used curse words.
2. Because he cut class, was disrespectful, and used curse words, I wrote a referral.

In the first sentence, the teacher is the focal point rather than the student and what he did to earn a referral. It is about the teacher's actions. Someone might even assume that this teacher had an axe to grind with the student because what the teacher did is the first thing the reader learns. In the second sentence, however, the focus is on what the student did, not on the teacher. It could even be argued that the positioning of the pronoun makes the statement appear more objective.

Using passive voice accomplishes a similar result, as in the following:

1. I expect you to turn in your lessons by the end of the week.
2. The expectation is that your lessons will be turned in by the end of the week.

Again, in the second sentence the emphasis is not on the teacher.

A skillful leader also uses diction that emphasizes where the onus of responsibility belongs. Compare these sentences:

1. You did not attend yesterday's meeting.
2. You chose not to attend yesterday's meeting.

By using the word "chose," the second sentence makes it clear that the person made a conscious decision not to attend the meeting, and it attempts to hold her accountable. The first statement, although accurate and perfectly acceptable, is not as strong.

Similarly, use words that reflect what actually occurred. For example, consider the following:

1. I gave him an *F* because of his low grades and incomplete work.
2. He earned an *F* because of his low grades and incomplete work.

In the first sentence, the focus is on the teacher, as I explained earlier, and the use of the word "gave," although technically correct, is not precise. In the second sentence—again the focus shifts to the student—the word "earn" is a better reflection of the situation.

Knowing the effect of certain punctuation devices is equally valuable. Note the use of the colon below:

1. Soon we will begin curriculum mapping.
2. Soon we will begin something that will have a positive influence on our students: curriculum mapping.

In the second example, suspense and heightened expectations are created because the reader must read further to determine exactly what the positive thing is. The colon supplies emphasis. Parenthetical phrases, on the other hand, lessen the importance of the information presented. A parenthetical aside (such as this) is not as strong as a declarative statement and should be avoided. Possessing such a solid grasp over the written word will work to a leader's advantage.

Documentation

Successful teachers who anticipate problems with parents begin early in the year by documenting a student's progress, behavior, and any related incident. These teachers arrive at a conference armed with papers, tests, and anecdotal notes as evidence to support their professional judgment and to safeguard against the highly sought after loophole. They make copies of letters sent home, and when they call parents, they record the day and time and with whom they spoke. An effective leader also recognizes the need to bulletproof himself by documenting his interactions with colleagues. He maintains a log of conversations and meetings so that he has his facts straight if a situation escalates.

Keep a written record of an event by following up with someone through e-mail or by summarizing something in an e-mail (Resource 11). Find a format or system for taking notes during a meeting: develop your own version of shorthand and then summarize the talking points of your meeting in an e-mail. Openly including others in an e-mail, such as your supervisors, makes them aware of a situation and protects you in case someone inquires about it. And it puts the recipient on alert because you are notifying others of the situation.

Before "bcc"-ing someone on an e-mail, check with her first to see how she feels about this option and to give her a heads-up that the e-mail is coming, so that she does not inadvertently hit the "Reply to All" button, which would expose her as a blind recipient. In addition, it is wise to save and to print sent and received e-mails in case some kind of documentation is needed in the future. In particularly problematic relationships, you might activate the read receipt option, which is a function that notifies you when the recipient has opened his e-mail, confirming it was actually received and not lost in cyberspace.

Oral Communication

Approach Your Team like Your Classroom.

When I became a department chair and had the opportunity to sit in a meeting from the other side of the proverbial desk, I realized how similar my department was to a classroom: the students were simply older. Some literature will outline different personality profiles by coining catchy names such as "The Motivator," "The Instigator," or "The Cheerleader," but it is just as easy to understand your team (and meetings) in terms of a classroom. Expect to have someone who is consistently tardy (with an excuse, no less), someone who is unprepared, someone who will stay after to discuss the meeting, someone who *must* have her voice heard, someone who will daydream, someone who wants to be there and someone who would rather be anywhere else, someone who will make wisecracks, someone who will complain about whatever is presented, someone who will be eager to hear what you have to say, and even someone who will talk and pass notes.

Understanding that these kinds of behaviors are comparable to your students' behaviors will give you greater insight into the group dynamics of your meetings and the personalities of your teachers, which will better help you to read them and know what to expect from them. Holding meetings will become much easier. But as an administrator warned me once I came to this realization, just because you recognize these personality types in your teachers, it does not mean that you should call them out. Nor should you address them the way you would address your students. You have to hope that your teachers will police one another so that you are not faced with the awkward decision of whether or not to do it yourself. If an incident occurs, consider speaking privately with the teacher after the meeting while the behavior is still fresh in your mind.

"How Do You Want to Handle This?"

Early in my tenure as department chair, I brought a situation to my administrator, and much to my surprise, he responded by asking, "How do you think you should handle it?" I was taken aback that someone in a supervisory position asked me what I thought. Even more surprising was that I had a solution, although I did not know it when I brought the situation to him; he was trying to help me realize it. It is easier and more efficient—but not more effective—to tell someone what to do, only that does not allow him to grow. As the old saying goes, "Catch a fish for a man and he eats for a day; teach him to fish and he eats for a lifetime." This administrator was trying to cultivate leadership skills in me that would help me survive on my own in the future.

Moreover, asking someone what he thinks of a situation automatically creates buy-in and it helps him understand that the problem is his, that you are there to help him solve it, not to take ownership of it. Asking "What do you think you should do?" nurtures people's instincts, builds their confidence that you are interested in their opinions, and provides you with an opportunity to guide them and help them grow as professionals. Asking a variation of this, "What do you want to see happen?" can also assist you. If it is apparent that your teacher does not have a solution but knows what outcome she wants, asking her this secures her permission and ensures that you won't be perceived as pushing your own agenda.

"What If?"

When a teacher brings you an idea or a proposal that you know is not feasible, don't squelch his enthusiasm by saying, "No, this won't work because . . ." For some reason, many people expect a negative response or an attack, which is why the saying "It's better to ask for forgiveness than for permission" is so prevalent in education. Set yourself up as an open-minded leader by agreeing to consider what he brings you. Put him at ease or disarm him by first listening to his idea without interrupting him. Then respond by asking, "What would happen if . . . ?" You won't be seen as negative or arrogant but instead as willing to brainstorm, helping him examine his idea from a different angle. You won't be the one responsible for saying no to something; ideally, he will be the one to realize it if his idea won't work. This reduces the possibility of having an acrimonious discussion or creating an adversarial relationship.

"Why Do You Ask?"

One administrator confirmed for me the effectiveness of responding to a question with a question. So when someone asks me a question, I try to respond with a question. For example, if a teacher says, "I get the feeling that you're upset with me—are you?" I try not to reply with a yes or no answer. That would limit the information I could potentially receive. Instead, responding with "Why do you ask?" buys me some time to assess the situation, to gauge how important the issue is to him. The responsibility then falls on him to explain his perceptions, and not on me to explain my feelings from the onset.

A similar technique would be asking "Why do you think that?" For example, a team leader came to me last year and said, "Kasey is pretty conservative with her assessments, isn't she?" I had thought that too, but I instead asked, "Why do you think that?" My team leader proceeded to confirm my thinking; I never once had to offer explicit information that I agreed. I encouraged her to work with this teacher by sharing ideas and activities, and she left the discussion feeling more valued for bringing the information to me.

Put It in the Positive.

Pretend a colleague accused you of being sarcastic. Your first reaction might be to defend yourself by replying, "No, I wasn't!" This is natural, and it is not wrong. But it creates the perception that you are defensive, maybe not open to criticism or hearing another's point of view. Instead, phrase your response in a positive manner, preferably in the form of a question because that might draw more information out of your colleague. Asking "I was?" is less defensive, which reduces the possibility of the other person becoming defensive. Whether you were sarcastic or not, asking him a question opens up the potential to discuss his perceptions further.

Similarly, instead of asking "Did you take care of that form that I asked you to?" it is more advantageous to couch your question in positive terms: "How did it go when you turned in that form?" This assumes the teacher has followed through on your request, and it places more of an onus of responsibility on him. By using this kind of questioning, you often are able to extract more than a simple yes or no answer. You can also cause the person to feel a little more pressure, even if that was not your intent. This, in turn, might better motivate him to follow through with his task because you had already assumed it had been taken care of and he won't want to let you down.

Don't Procrastinate.

If at some point it is necessary to meet with one of your teachers, don't put it off. Think about what happens when a teacher has a disruptive or an underachieving student and waits a couple of months to call home about an issue that had been present since the beginning of the year. The parents are bewildered and frustrated because they were not made aware of the situation earlier. The delay in contacting them can make rectifying the problem more difficult. The same holds true for your teachers. If there is a problem, odds are it will not correct itself, and the longer you delay, the larger, more far-reaching, and less palatable the problem becomes.

If you put off these discussions because you believe they will be confrontational and you are uncomfortable with confrontation, find ways to make the meeting nonconfrontational. Meet in the workroom instead of your classroom so that you are in neutral territory, or meet in your teacher's classroom to minimize defensiveness. Don't barricade yourself behind a desk; consider sitting at an angle, side by side, rather than across from each other. And as you would in a parent conference, always try to find something positive to say at the end of the dialogue, lessening the chance that the other person will walk away feeling beaten down.

"What Did You Learn?"

It's odd that as educators we are so obsessed with what our students have learned, whether they succeeded or failed, but we sometimes forget to reflect and evaluate ourselves, let alone encourage our peers to do so. As a teacher leader, you have innumerable responsibilities and demands on your time, so it is natural to forget about the growth of your teachers. However, discussing their experiences in the classroom, after parent conferences, and after meetings with administrators is a key aspect to developing leadership skills, both theirs and yours. Have them reflect on a meeting and ask them questions that will help them learn from it:

- Were you pleased with how it went? Why or why not?
- Which behaviors would you want to model? Why?
- What do you wish you had done differently?
- What do you wish the other person had done differently?
- What did you learn about the other person based on his responses and behavior?
- What did you learn from the experience and how will you apply it in the future?
- What are your goals for the next time?

Practice Active Questioning.

Let your school and all its potential scenarios be your classroom.

There is an abundance of literature that promotes "active listening," and correctly so. While these advocates believe that leaders should try to be as quiet as possible so that they can fully hear what their colleagues are saying, they also stress the value of asking questions to get to the heart of the matter. Based on the latter, it is sometimes more accurate to call this technique "active questioning," because you are asking penetrating questions to ascertain what your colleagues actually mean. Asking "Are you saying that . . . ?" "Am I correct in paraphrasing what you said as . . . ?" "Can you clarify what you mean?" or "I'm not entirely clear—can you rephrase what you just said?" forces the speaker to clarify his statements and views, which helps to avoid future confusion and allows you to box a teacher in when you need to.

Be Responsive.

When I was searching for ways to be a better department chair, I talked with many teachers across grade levels and discovered that one of their main concerns occurred when leaders—teacher leaders and administrators—superficially treated a worry, problem, or complaint. Because teachers drop everything for their students, in many ways they want their leader to respond to them in a similar fashion. Obviously this is not always possible, but it is good advice to guide you in your interactions with your teachers. I know one leader who would pay more attention to the work in front of him than to the teacher trying to talk with him. Writing an e-mail from time to time while a teacher is talking with you might be necessary for efficiency, and it might be acceptable when we know the issue is not an urgent one. It is unacceptable when this kind of behavior dominates all interactions, however, as was the case with this leader. Teachers never felt they had his attention because he only seemed to perfunctorily give them his time.

Worse yet is flippantly responding to a concern, failing to understand why an issue is important, or not following up on a problem. An ill-placed joke to lighten the mood can express a lack of interest in what someone else is interested in. Instead, leaders need to be responsive. They need to know their teachers well enough to determine when they truly feel passionate about something versus when they are annoyed. If you don't understand why something is significant to your teachers, ask them to explain their feelings. Find a way to relate. Sometimes sympathy can be more valuable than producing results. Finally, be sure to follow through with and follow up on situations. Even if you are unable to bring about the resolution that your teacher is hoping for, your persistence, dedication, and advocacy will be remembered in the long run.

Build Your Network.

As a department chair, there will be many times when you cannot go to your teachers for advice or input, no matter how much you trust them. You might not be able to go to your administrator either because you can't always bother him with every little issue that comes up (or perhaps he is part of the situation). But if you are able to establish and nurture positive, trusting relationships with other teacher leaders in your building, you will have people to get advice from and to bounce ideas off of.

These leaders can play a vital role in improving your team because they are objective and not personally involved with issues that you might bring them. As a result, they might be able to offer insight and strategies for handling problems that you are blind to because you are so closely involved. In addition, this creates an outlet for you and the other teacher leaders to safely vent frustrations instead of simmering over them, which can adversely affect your team, not to mention your personal life.

Another advantage to having such a network is that it can be a resource. If you are short on supplies and have a limited budget for purchasing them, you might be able to barter with another chair for additional supplies. For example, when I need specific supplies immediately and am unable to wait for them to arrive, I obtain them from chairs by trading for future supplies or in exchange for editing something that they need to send out to parents. Furthermore, if you are close with other chairs, organizations and committees that you serve on (such as an instructional council) are more likely to be more cohesive, unified, and productive. Chairs will end up supporting other departments instead of trying to sink them. And there might be a trickle-down effect in terms of increased collegiality and collaboration among teachers in various departments.

Nonverbal Communication

Facial Expressions

Even though we might say one thing, our facial expressions can betray our true feelings. We might meet with a colleague who we are not especially fond of and our feelings unintentionally come across through our facial expressions. We might meet with an administrator and claim to agree with something but our expressions tell him otherwise. We might profess patience and interest, but our demeanor screams irritation and indifference. These are difficult things to control, but they need to be addressed. A good poker player will pick up on a "tell" or figure out when someone is bluffing, and so will your colleagues.

If you are unaware of such tells, ask a trusted colleague to observe you during a meeting to see if you have any. I never thought my tells were obvious until I had a talk with another department chair after a meeting, and she commented that she noticed me repeatedly clenching my jaw when I became frustrated. Although I pretended patience and said all the right things, my teeth grinding indicated otherwise. I asked her to observe me at the next meeting to see what else I unknowingly did. A good acting coach does the same thing: he will study his subjects to determine what mannerisms and ticks they have and correct them. If you have ever videotaped yourself teaching, you will understand what I am saying about certain mannerisms and tells.

Similarly, you should study the facial expressions of the people you work with and come to understand what they mean. What tells do they have? Does she gesticulate while talking? Does he stroke his beard while thinking? What does such behavior signify? When are colleagues saying one thing but expressing another? By paying attention to facial expressions and other nonverbal cues, you'll be able to better deal and communicate with your colleagues as well as to read them.

Body Language

We are often quick to pick up on a student's body language and discern its meaning. Is he looking at the ground? Avoiding eye contact? Standing with his arms folded across his chest? Slouched in his seat? But sometimes when it comes to working with adults, we miss vital body language clues simply because we are working with adults. We detect the meaning of signs when they are blatant, but at that point it may be too late for us to take proactive measures.

Worse yet, we often exhibit negative body language ourselves that we may not even be aware of. I knew teachers who were uncomfortable approaching their department chair because he never seemed to be able to look his female teachers in the eye; his eyes kept wandering slightly south of their chins. If he had been aware of this kind of behavior and avoided it, perhaps he would have been a stronger leader and his teachers would have trusted him more. Another department chair had the habit of folding her arms, whether she was standing or sitting. She wasn't cross with the people who approached her; this was simply a position that was comfortable to her. Unfortunately, it took teachers a few months to realize that she was not irritable, that she was not annoyed with them, before any real productive meetings could occur. Therefore, be conscious of how you sit, stand, or approach people because even what we might consider benign body language has the potential to be misinterpreted.

Actions

As the cliché goes, actions speak louder than words. What we do or how we act in front of our teachers can strengthen their confidence in us and inspire them to follow us (and the converse is equally true). Demonstrating content knowledge earns respect, but action can make a quicker, more powerful statement.

On the initial inservice day during my first week as department chair, one of my first interactions with a teacher concerned the master schedule. An administrator was going to change her schedule before school started, for seemingly arbitrary reasons. The two of us met with him regarding the situation. Although I understood his reasons for the change, I did not think it made enough sense to disrupt her schedule and, by extension, at least one other teacher's schedule. When I mentioned this to him, he exclaimed, "If I want to, I can give her four preps!" I responded, "You're in charge of the schedule, so you certainly can . . . but how will burning this teacher out before the first quarter ends be in the best interest of the students?"

Even though I responded calmly and logically, I knew I was putting myself in danger by questioning his decision. But I also knew the background on my teacher; I needed to demonstrate my leadership to her as soon as possible. Advocating for her seemed the best way to earn credibility. The administrator's proposed change was never made, and I earned my teacher's respect in the process.

Teacher leaders can set a strong example by bringing about change, working on behalf of students and teachers, and showing that leadership is not always taxing but often rewarding. Sometimes, if we are lucky enough, our actions can even motivate our teachers to pursue future leadership positions.

The Communication Gap

Why are we meeting? Why did he say that? What did he mean by that? Why exactly are we doing this? Communication in all its forms is generally sorely lacking in schools. Whether it is because teachers and administrators are too busy to say what they mean and mean what they say, or because we assume too much, or even because some are just poor communicators, the communication gap exists in almost all school buildings. One of teachers' greatest frustrations is being ill informed or not receiving information in a timely fashion. Therefore, make bridging the communication gap one of your main priorities.

Find ways to keep your teachers informed and knowledgeable. Just as you would announce assignments to your students several times, remind your teachers in different ways at different intervals of upcoming meeting or due dates. Send e-mail, leave notes in teachers' in-boxes, tack announcements on bulletin boards, use routing slips (where information is sent from teacher to teacher and each person initials that she received the material and then passes it along to the next teacher on the list), and write newsletters. I also use slightly unconventional techniques—posting information on bathroom doors, mirrors, and computer monitors—to better ensure that people will find the necessary information.

Holding Meetings

Sometimes it feels as if we have meetings because we are expected to have them. If a meeting was 20 minutes long, teachers complain that it was a waste of time. If it was an hour and 20 minutes long, they complain that presenting the information in a handout could have shortened the meeting. Many meetings seem this way (faculty meetings can be the biggest culprits). It's not that people don't want to give up their time; teachers are the most self-sacrificing professionals who exist. Rather, it's that they want their time together to be meaningful and productive.

Few things are more demoralizing than showing up to a meeting excited to be with and work with colleagues only to have a leader read information *at* you. Often the information is read verbatim as it appears on the agenda. This sucks the life out of any meeting and reduces what might have been a professional atmosphere into a bureaucratic (and insulting) one. One department chair, although respected, often found her department meetings to be lethargic and marked by low attendance. The agenda items and statements were merely read aloud with no extrapolation whatsoever. This offends teachers, because we all know how to read, and we know our time could be better spent doing more pressing things.

Use your time together more efficiently. General information should be disseminated through e-mail or as an addendum to the agenda that people can read on their own. When possible, distribute the agenda to your team before the meeting. Set a time limit for each agenda item and, if practical, give a brief synopsis of each item so that people can come prepared to discuss or work on an item (Resource 12). Document your meetings by having someone take minutes, allowing members to revise the minutes within a certain time period, and then making the minutes accessible to everyone. Minutes should list who was present, absent, or late. They should document topics and issues (what was discussed), outcomes and resolutions (what was decided), and only what occurred during the meeting, not something that occurred before or after (Resource 13).

One of the most important things you can do is establish ground rules for your meetings. At the beginning of the school year, effective teachers collaborate with students to build community and determine the ground rules for their classes: how will classes be organized, what are the routines and procedures, what are the rules. Do the same with your teachers. Every year I begin my first department meeting by determining what our meeting start time will be. I ask my teachers if they would rather start soon after the school day ends so we can finish earlier, or if they want more time between the final bell and the meeting, which then affects how late they are in the building. I also determine how teachers feel about having a working lunch; if we only need to meet for 20 or 30 minutes, having a working lunch is sometimes more agreeable than meeting after school.

A regular meeting time and place are necessary; people become frustrated if the rules of the game keep changing. Because most people are creatures of habit, and because teachers face so much uncertainty over the course of their day, it's good to have one thing that is a constant. Some may contend that rotating meeting locations through different rooms is beneficial because it allows teachers to see what others are doing in their classes. However, having a consistent site might be more helpful, because it is one less thing for teachers to have to keep track of. And if your team functions in a professional manner, members would routinely be in other rooms picking up ideas. Moreover, if you are the team leader or department chair, having a consistent location will be helpful as you deal with your many obligations.

Much like students during a class discussion, teachers need to feel that they are "safe" in your meetings, that they can express their feelings or opinions without repercussions. The bulk of this responsibility falls on you. You need to ensure that people can have their voices heard. Although each teacher is a valuable addition to a team, to validate all contributions, as some advise, can be counterproductive and patronizing. Rather, it is the team member's willingness to contribute that should be valued.

In turn, you need to help your teachers understand the importance of an open atmosphere. For example, early in my first year as department chair, a meeting was becoming unproductive because people were talking over one another, not listening to each other, cutting each other off, and the like. At the next department meeting, I held off with my agenda and instead initiated a discussion on what constitutes effective versus ineffective meetings (Resource 14).

Being open about shortcomings allowed us to rectify them. Some teachers expressed their frustration with several teachers showing up late to meetings. We agreed that we wouldn't punish those who were professional enough to be there on time by delaying the start of the meeting. Some were troubled by our inability to communicate well: a couple of teachers were engaging in side conversations, one was trying to grade papers, and another seemed compelled to always make a joke. In this case, we briefly discussed professional behavior and expectations and expressed our recommitment to one another. There were also concerns about teachers who spoke for too long or parroted what others had already said. One teacher suggested imposing a time limit on how long someone could hold the floor. Another, using *Lord of the Flies* as inspiration, recommended that only the person holding the "conch" should be recognized.

I simply listened to these suggestions: I never offered my opinion on what I thought would or wouldn't work. I merely guided my team through the discussion. By the end of the meeting, every teacher was in agreement with a colleague's proposal that a parliamentarian was needed to recognize who had the floor, to move discussions forward, and to stop us from repeating what had already been covered. Although these issues were important to me, what was more important was making sure that it was my teachers' decision and a decision that all would be able to support.

You should also involve your team in determining how decisions are made. Is a majority vote or a two-thirds vote used? Under what circumstances do you, as leader, make a decision, and when does the entire team have a voice? Is a quorum needed to vote on an item? What constitutes a quorum? Can a teacher vote on behalf of a colleague who is absent? Establishing such ground rules will make it easier for you to run more effective meetings.

Finally, make your meetings productive: transform your department into a learning department rather than letting it stagnate as a bureaucratic department. How long a meeting lasts is not something that your teachers can necessarily have input on, but you should keep in mind that adults are just like students: we can have short attention spans. As I'm sure you have heard or seen, teachers can be worse than their students at meetings. So with that in mind, vary your activities and discussion topics, and try not to have meetings that last for more than an hour. If a lengthy meeting is unavoidable, provide your teachers with breaks. But always ask yourself why you are meeting—for them or for me? You should gather for a clear purpose, a purpose that could not be accomplished through an e-mail or a memo, and you should make sure that your teachers know what it is.

Setting Goals

Regardless of the type of leadership position you hold, your group needs to come to some kind of agreement concerning its goals. The group's goals and expectations should be clear and realistic. When I became chair, it would have been unrealistic, and unreasonable, for me or for anyone else to expect the department to increase our 73 percent passing rate by 25 percent. But to simply say that "we will be better" or "we will improve our scores" is vague. You must be able to measure your achievement. You might have an incredible team and as a result believe that you can improve standardized scores by 15

Goals need to be realistic, achievable, and measurable.

percent, but to state so in a work plan might set you up for failure. Lowballing your expectations might be the safer bet (just as you might have hoped for a *C* on a test and then been pleasantly surprised when you pulled an *A*).

Goals should be agreed upon rather than handed down by you because you need to have buy-in. If you present data that show a large percentage of your students missing test questions related to certain objectives, then it should be tacitly understood that this is an area that needs improvement and hence is a goal. All teachers should have input in drafting a strategy for reaching goals, which I call a GoalAction, and in establishing a realistic, flexible timeline (Resource 15). If the goal is to raise standardized test scores by 5 percent, that obviously can only be measured at the end of the year. However, that does not mean a team cannot assess its progress before then.

A team should set target dates throughout the year so that it can reflect and analyze its headway. To facilitate reflection on progress, a team leader should administer a status report and make such reports available to administrators (Resource 16). Data acquired from a midterm examination can be compared against pre-tests and quarter grades. If the data reveal that advancement is not being made, or not being made as rapidly as originally planned, the strategy might need to be revised and the target dates altered.

As famed coach of the Green Bay Packers Vince Lombardi believed, "Individual commitment to a group effort is what makes a team work, a company work, a civilization work" (Phillips, 2002, p. 24). So if you want your team to be effective, each member must be committed toward the cause or goal. Those who are not are a drain on time and resources and will prevent the team from achieving success. These people cannot be allowed to drag the team in different directions, either by hijacking meetings to discuss or promote their own interests or by working against the goal.

For instance, as much as some teachers loathe high-stakes testing and believe it reduces education to skill-and-drill or adversely affects students, their priority, their responsibility, even their legal obligation is to ensure that students possess the knowledge and skills necessary to pass those tests. Opponents need to be converted or convinced. We are hired to teach the local and county objectives, so we must be committed to them, whether we believe in them or not. This is the core of our contracts.

People must also be committed to open dialogue. Nothing is accomplished when we withhold how we feel. Colleagues should not be attacked, but ideas can be. True, some believe that if their idea is attacked, then it is an attack on them. In a team's inchoate stages, this is to be expected. But team building is one way to alleviate this problem, and being cognizant of our tone, what we say, and how we phrase it is another way.

In order for you to be a successful leader, your team needs to be clear not only on its goals but also on why the team exists. For example, during the first four or five months I served on the Instructional Council, a leadership and decision-making group composed of the instructional leaders in my building, I had a vague idea of why we existed: to address instructional matters. But what were those instructional matters? Where were they defined? What shouldn't we address? What couldn't we address? Although we were all instructional leaders, what were our roles within this group? And how would we know when we were overstepping our bounds and infringing on the authority of others?

Consumed by questions and confusion, I sought clarification, but all I could learn was that "we are the Instructional Council." Attending interminable meetings without clear agendas, timelines, procedures, or goals and without a clearly defined common purpose, I found our time together extremely frustrating. From conversations with other members, I learned that they were equally exasperated.

To avoid such counterproductivity, your team must decide where it is heading and what roles are needed to move it forward. If you all board a train but have different ideas of where it should head, you will end up spinning your wheels on the tracks, as we did that year. On the Instructional Council, some teachers felt our job was to deal with organizational leadership—deciding which groups could take field trips and when—while others thought our purpose was to focus on staff development and instructional leadership. Still other leaders thought we had "too much power" and should act only on direction from the principal. We had 22 leaders who were all leading, or, more accurately, pulling in different directions. At best, we were not as effective as we could be, and, at worst, we were downright ineffectual.

My experience on the Instructional Council made me realize the importance of a mission statement. If your group can come to consensus on its objective and create procedures and ground rules, then you will ease the strain of your journey. Teachers' strengths will be maximized, because you will all be proceeding toward a common destination.

Drafting a Mission Statement

A mission statement does not need to be elaborate—the more cumbersome the statement, the more likely it is that people will not remember any of it—nor should it be rigid, because an organization's needs can alter over time. When I created my first department meeting agenda, I titled it "Mission Possible" to signify that it was possible for us to be extraordinary teachers and have high-achieving students in a school that had been largely forgotten by the community, educators, and politicians. We set a positive tenor by succinctly summarizing that we could meet the challenges of the state's barrier tests.

A year later, we had achieved success: Mission Accomplished. We had sidestepped failure, so we expanded our horizons while sharpening our purpose:

> The Falls Church High School English Department will develop and encourage independent learners who demonstrate analytical and critical thinking skills in a standards-based classroom that focuses on essential knowledge. We will foster mastery and fluency of Standard English communication through a variety of literature and its appreciation.

My teachers knew that "hobby teaching," as an administrator put it (valuing and teaching certain passions over prescribed curriculum and mandates), had been prevalent in the past. So it was important to come to agreement and announce what we valued and that we were committed to helping our students meet standards (albeit political ones). We understood that this had been our objective a year earlier, but given the climate and pressure at the time to achieve standardized success, it was better to distill it to "Mission Possible." Once we had met our goals, however, it was essential for us to sit down and elaborate on our purpose. The same holds true for any other department or team of teachers. The slippery part is creating a mission statement.

A mission statement should focus on your goals, on what you intend to accomplish rather than on theories.

When creating the department's mission statement, it was imperative to ensure consensus. One person alone could not dictate what our statement said. I divided the room in half and gave each side poster paper so we could write down what we believed our goals were. Twenty minutes later, we taped the sheets of poster paper to the wall and looked for common phrases, which were then recorded on the chalkboard. After much discussion over single words, we turned the thoughts and fragments into sentences. We analyzed our statement to determine if it truly captured what we believed in and made corrections, revisions, and decisions as a large group.

Instead of calling for a vote on the statement, I used the fist-five technique—teachers held up five fingers if they completely agreed with the statement, three fingers if they did not completely agree with it but could live with it, or their closed fist if they were opposed and could not live with it. Rather than creating winners and losers by voting through a majority rules process, this technique allowed people to express their concerns and enabled us to address those concerns, which better ensured consensus.

When it came to achieving consensus with the Instructional Council, I found a different technique to be more beneficial because we were a larger group. We broke into pairs and jotted down ideas on four index cards. After a few minutes of comparing notes and discussing our choices, we eliminated dissimilar ideas. Pairs then joined up with other pairs to narrow down the number of cards they held, either by finding common ground or discarding ideas that were different. The narrowing down continued until the entire group was working with a common vocabulary or we were satisfied with the remaining cards. Both processes allowed every person to have input. If someone was adamant about a particular phrase, it did not need to be discounted, as it would have been if we had gone for a strict majority vote.

A mission statement can be a powerful tool for conveying your vision, building consensus, and demonstrating your leadership. Once you've become a more effective communicator and bridged the communication gap in your school, you will be better positioned to bring about change and positively influence student achievement, the true charge of teacher leadership.

References

Phillips, D. (2002). *Run to win: Vince Lombardi on coaching and leadership.* New York: St. Martin's.

4

Adaptive Leadership

Navigating Challenges and Effecting Change

Even though teachers are natural leaders every day in their classrooms, they have never truly been viewed in that way, which may cause anxiety and apprehension for administrators. Some administrators—perhaps those who still adhere to the formal one-person, or classical, model of leadership—might not be comfortable with moving away from practices that they are familiar or comfortable with. If you face administrative resistance and reluctance, your chances of succeeding are greatly diminished. Administrators are under pressure, and the natural inclination of some might be to curtail leadership because they are directly responsible for improving achievement and reluctant to relinquish control. Therefore, you need to become your own best advocate for increased involvement.

Yet as a leader you might face significant teacher resistance as well. Teachers might perceive that the decision-making process is being manipulated and massaged by the administration or that your motives aren't true, causing them to further distrust chairs or to view them as obstructions. Some might feel envious and jealous that a colleague is in a position of leadership or influence, while others might be cynical and wary of a colleague with increased authority. Unfortunately, there is little you can do to assuage those who are resentful of your activity and your interest in safeguarding or enhancing the well-being of your school. But show your teachers that the best way to move forward is by equipping all with leadership skills and opportunities, and find ways to prevent them from feeling alienated, isolated, or fearful.

Working with Your Administrator

Those in leadership positions must understand their responsibilities and boundaries and be wary of overstepping them. Perhaps more than most professionals, teachers are extremely territorial. If they do step on someone else's toes, and it was in the best interest of a student, it is usually forgivable. But the teacher leader who intrudes on an administrator's turf is usually not easily forgiven.

Sometimes administrators will cut a teacher leader out of the loop because they see him as one more person they need to deal with. Ostensibly this makes sense for them, but it can foster the belief that the administration is autocratic or that it does not truly support its teachers. Ultimately, this will have an adverse effect on morale and climate, so you should find a way to let administrators involve you.

Develop a relationship with your administrator that is not based solely on putting out fires.

If you desire more responsibility and a greater voice, you need to earn your administrator's trust. You need to demonstrate that you are competent enough to take on certain tasks, and you need to show that you are willing to be challenged. Being a solid instructional leader, exhibiting a good track record, or just being reliable can help accomplish this. A strong work ethic can develop a rapport with your administrator to the point that she trusts you and is confident granting you autonomy. Administrators prefer working with someone who has a strong work ethic; if necessary, they can teach leadership skills.

Although most administrators were once teachers themselves, they put much stock in their authority and have the power to support it as well. A healthy dose of caution and respect is in order. It is possible to unintentionally and unknowingly harm yourself with your interactions with administrators, and doing so obviously carries far-reaching and more dangerous repercussions than if you were to do the same with your teachers. Whereas the information I have presented up to this point is mainly geared toward working with your fellow teachers, the same can hold true for how you approach your administrator. But, as I illustrate below, there are a host of additional things to consider.

Pick Which Sword to Fall On.

A principal once told me that I had the habit of being "dead right." I was pleased to hear her say that because I had been toiling to raise scores and solve institutional problems, so I was glad that she had noticed. She let me bask in her comment before she elaborated; it was not the accolade I thought it was. She explained that at times I was like a car trying to pass a truck, which always carries a certain amount of risk. The truck begins to move into my lane without signaling, and I refuse to yield because I have the right of way. Holding my position, I am forced off the road and die. I was right, but it was an empty victory. As she described, I was dead right.

Many teachers and teacher leaders fall prey to this kind of behavior. We're quick to criticize administrators for not taking the action that we believe to be the best, and we accuse them, directly or otherwise, of being weak, unsupportive leaders. In some cases, we know we are right. Consequently, we try to be ethical, have integrity, and uphold standards. However, there are times, whether we admit it or not, that we do not have an understanding of the bigger picture or the ramifications of what we want.

Regardless, you first need to remember the following: your administrator is your superior. You might not agree with her rationale for a decision, but you are required to respect it. Perhaps the most difficult thing for a teacher leader is to admit that he is wrong. As much as we like to think we know everything, our administrators generally have more experience. Moreover, a decision we disagree with might not even come from them. It could be a product of community, county, or school board pressure, and, as a result, administrators have to support it. Just as we teachers sometimes receive a mandate we don't necessarily agree with but must respect, the same holds true for administrators. The difference is that they might not have the luxury to express their disagreement or even to acknowledge the source of a directive.

So as a teacher leader, you need to carefully determine if you are willing to die for your cause. There are several swords in your building, some hidden and some not, but all dangerously, and perhaps fatally, sharp. Which one are you willing to fall on? Sometimes we don't see the blood or realize that we have already fallen on a sword until it's too late. It's good to fight for what you believe in or for what you know is right, but if you do so every time, you will quickly die on the battlefield and be of no help to anyone. Before deciding to move ahead with an issue with your supervisor, it is always wise to consider the following:

- How important is this issue to my teacher or to me?
- What is the root cause of this issue or where did it originate?
- How might this affect my teacher or me in the long run?
- How might this affect my/our relationship with the administrator?
- Am I prepared to face the consequences of being right?
- Am I doing this for the right reasons?
- Will my involvement complicate or help matters?
- If I choose not to push the issue, will my teachers understand and still respect me? Will I be able to live with myself as a professional, as a leader?

Let Others Discover That the Stove Is Hot.

I made a crucial mistake when I told an assistant principal on his second day of work, "There are some problem areas that you should be aware of, so can we touch base right now about them?" Timing aside, I did not give him a chance to feel out the situation for himself. I was basically telling him, before I even knew him, that I did not trust him to figure out things on his own.

Instead, I should have said, "There are some problem areas that you should be aware of, so after you get acclimated, let's sit down and compare notes." The second statement affords him respect and dignity while informing him that issues need to be addressed. Just as you wouldn't want to bias a new teacher with information about her incoming students, you should give your administrator a chance to form his own opinions.

Don't Blindside Your Supervisor.

This might appear to contradict the above advice, but the reality is that working with administrators can be precarious. When are you giving them too little information? Too much information? What information do you keep to yourself? Which situations do you handle yourself? When do you involve them in a problem? Unfortunately, there is no easy answer because many times the situation dictates the solution. But a good general rule of thumb is never let your administrator be blindsided.

As an administrator once told me, he would rather hear about a situation or a problem from me than from a parent. Or worse yet, from his supervisor. Again, as with dealing with your students' parents, don't delay in making your administrator aware of things. You don't necessarily need to meet over every single issue, but it is a good idea to copy him on an e-mail regarding a situation that could potentially pose problems, or to touch base with him about a brewing situation that could boil over. A deluge of e-mails may frustrate him because of the time involved in sifting through them, but it is better to cover yourself (which is often the name of the game) than to be left exposed to future questioning.

Ask for Help.

We frequently receive unreasonable goals or mandates. We stress over them and beat our brains to find a way to make things happen, even when we feel that we are being asked the impossible.

Instead of inflicting this kind of silent torture on yourself when an administrator hands down a request, ask him how he would approach it. We are rarely able to question mandates because they often come from outside the building, so don't ignore the opportunity to talk with the person making the difficult request.

If you ask for help, administrators will appreciate it: they want to feel needed. We are quick to assume that a teacher became an administrator because he hated the classroom or couldn't cut it as a teacher. This is not usually the case, and administrators should be respected as leaders. Involve them. They may ask how you would handle it, but bring it back to them to see what they would suggest. Try to have them share ownership of a request that you believe you are unable to deliver on. If they have no help to offer, that in and of itself might be telling. Don't let it end there. Schedule an appointment to meet again to brainstorm solutions.

Evolve.

If a new administrator enters the building, you might not be able to function exactly as you did with your previous administrator. You must demonstrate adaptive leadership. If you plan to remain in your leadership position, you need to determine your administrator's goals and vision and find a way to have yours match his. Determine his philosophy and leadership style. What kind of leader is he? Does your style of leadership mesh with his? If not, how can you alter your philosophy and style so that you are still true to what you believe but at the same time are able to work effectively with him? If you don't consider these things and find solutions, you will render yourself obsolete.

Be the Good Cop.

No one likes to be the bad guy. Children understand this, which is why they go to one parent for something when they already know or sense that the other won't grant it. Similarly, as a colleague once explained to me, when it comes to working with your administrator, you need to have a relationship like those on police dramas: good cop, bad cop. Teacher leaders have authority, but we do not have power. Our positions can create authority, but ultimately it is respect that motivates our teachers to work with us. There is very little we can do to get our teachers to act how we want or how they should. That is the job of an administrator. It is his role to bring the hammer down when necessary, not yours.

Playing the part of bad cop will be more damaging to you than your administrator because you work so closely with your teachers. So that leaves you with the role of good cop. If your administrator is uncomfortable with being the bad cop, keep playing good cop but keep bringing her information. Make her aware of a situation—so that you cannot be held responsible for it—and eventually it will reach the point where she won't be able to ignore it.

Show the Barometer.

Sometimes administrators are so inundated with the demands, threats, and needs of students and parents that they do not have the time to remember what it was like in the classroom. Understandably, they can forget the most essential element to achievement: the well-being of the teacher. In the current frenzy of high-stakes testing and accountability, teachers are stressed, overworked, and underappreciated. And an administrator who has been out of the classroom for many years might not fully realize how much more challenging it has become to be a successful teacher. Help him understand what it is like to be in the classroom in the climate of high-stakes testing, in the culture of the instant gratification generation, in the age of the absolution of responsibility. Let him know when morale is down and why. For example, you might need to tell him that someone needs a thank-you or a supportive voice because her plate is overloaded.

Foster an Honest Relationship.

An administrator may not be able to discuss legal issues with you or everything that crosses his desk, but if you are bringing him news, issues, and information, you need, and should expect, him to behave in a similar fashion. Find a way to get him to treat you with the same respect that you afford him by being a forthright and trusting leader. Demonstrate through your actions that you can be trusted. Keep confidential information to yourself. Know when to pry or push and know when to let sleeping dogs lie.

Above all, be direct. We want our teachers and students to be direct with us, and we should be equally straightforward with our administrator. Let him know how you feel if you are cut out of the loop. Direct questions have a way of unnerving people, but if you ask them in a respectful, professional manner, and in the best interest of your teachers and students, a good administrator should be willing to discuss his reasons for including or excluding you. If he still isn't forthcoming with information, analyze each situation and present the reasons why you should be included. Explain to him how your being in the loop will benefit him and make his job easier.

Sometimes it is not even about being included; it can simply be about being informed. At an Instructional Council meeting, several department chairs expressed their concerns about overcrowded classes and a lack of desks to accommodate the increase in students. Before an administrator could respond, one chair proclaimed that we as chairs did not need to know about everything that was going on in the school, that it was not our place to know. On the surface, her comment has a shade of truth to it, but such a mentality fosters distrust. I replied that if we aren't informed well enough to respond to teacher concerns, as in this case regarding class sizes, gossip then rules the school. Teachers are quick to spread their own theories or to jump on the smallest bit of information that someone might provide and trumpet it as fact. This adversely affects morale and climate.

Open and honest communication is the remedy; it makes us stronger and more effective. The administrator was surprised because he thought that we already knew the reasons and had passed them on to our teachers, and I believe he recognized through the ensuing discussion the importance of cultivating communication and granting access to information. Likewise, it is essential that you are open and honest with your administrator. Don't cover up mistakes, don't keep information from him, and don't lie to him. Your administrator will eventually find out whatever it is you're being deceptive about, so be as upfront and honest as possible.

Make Your Supervisor Look Good.

One of your myriad responsibilities as a leader is to make your supervisor look good. Although it sounds unfair, that is the name of the game. We see this in the business world where the common worker toils so his company can increase its profit margin, and, when it does, the executive is rewarded with a large year-end bonus. We see this in school systems where administrators and central office personnel are rewarded for improving test scores. Your administrator may even end up receiving all the credit initially for the good things you have done with your department, team, or program. So be it. Continue to do what you have done; eventually you will receive the recognition you deserve. You must remember that when your administrator looks good, you look good. After all, you want your team to make you look good, and you should set the example by your interactions with those above you.

In addition, you should be a watchdog for your administrator. Be his backstop and catch his mistakes. Never show him up or publicly criticize or disagree with him. It's not your job to convince him that you are right; your first responsibility is to find a way to support him. In some cases, you might need to work a conversation so that by the end of it, he believes that he came up with the solution, idea, or proposal.

Leading When Some Don't Want to Follow

Every committee, grade level, team, department, and school has someone who will vigorously resist any kind of change. It may be the teacher who feels that "this proposal is just another fad" or that "this too shall pass." Education reform is often cyclical, or at least borrows heavily from the past, so many teachers are skeptical about the efficacy of a "new" idea. They are resistant because they believe that they have seen it before, that "it didn't work then and it won't work now." Or, like most people, they fear change, and they panic over having to move outside their comfort zone.

Others will resist change simply because it comes from you. If you were promoted from within, some teachers may resent you for advancing in a career that offers very little advancement. They may feel that *they* deserve the position, even if they didn't inquire about it or apply for it. They may have been your friends at some point but now see you as a traitor or a sellout, closely aligned with the administration because you are in a position of leadership. It will be difficult to convince them otherwise, so just continue treating them fairly and standing up for what you believe in.

If you were brought in from out of house—from a different school or school system—you will surely face some resistance. You'll be seen as an intruder who has entered a close-knit family, especially if the teachers had no voice in the matter. "But she does not know anything about our kids," "Our school is unique," or "It's going to take us time to train him" are comments people frequently make when they fear that someone is poised to initiate change or disrupt their comfortable quiet. Probably the most familiar line is "I was here before her and I'll be here after her." People who believe this are prepared to survive the meltdown. And in worse cases, they will initiate one. They will hunker down and use all the resources of the informal power structure to ensure their survival while plotting your demise.

Leading during a period of success is relatively easy. It is how we deal with adversity, challenges, and change that shows our mettle—or if there is inconsistency between what we preach and what we practice. In the face of resistance and obstacles, we discover that we are leaders or that we need to learn how to become leaders. The question is how best to approach challenging situations. Do you need to convert those who oppose you? How do you find a way to work with these people? How do you move ahead with change?

Don't Tip Your Hand.

Before I was introduced to my department in May, my administrator warned me about a teacher who had declared that she was going to "see how much he knows." He told me that he wanted to be present at this meeting in case her cross-examination of me became too belligerent. Sure enough, as soon as I had finished introducing myself and my credentials, this teacher, with folded arms, coldly asked, "What are your goals for the department?" Instead of rattling off a list of things that I thought should be changed, I politely replied, "Well, what do *you* think the goals should be?" She seemed shocked by my question, and nearly a minute elapsed while she tried to stammer out an answer. I didn't leave her on the hook too long and reclaimed the floor, stating that test scores were the obvious concern of the administration and county, so we needed to examine those.

This strategy at my first meeting was crucial: I didn't lay my cards on the table. Although my main purpose in turning the question back on her was to send the implicit message that I was not going to bullied, it also served to show others that I was interested in hearing what they had to say. My general answer prevented me from painting myself into a corner with a statement that could be held against me later. Because I did not immediately present changes or proposals, the meeting did not have a chance to get acrimonious, and I avoided setting myself up for a barrage of questions, challenges, and complaints. Moreover, I did not say anything about imminent changes that would have sparked anxiety in the room.

After the meeting ended, I spoke with individuals in hopes of gauging how they felt about some of the things that I knew needed to be changed. Much to my surprise, I discovered they were pleased that I had "turned the tables" on this teacher, because she had a reputation for bullying others and anointing herself the intellectual superior of the department. Her visible loss for words dimmed the aura of power she had created for herself. Others were pleased by my response because they saw it as a sign that I was a leader who would seek and encourage input.

Sit on Your Hands.

One mistake that new leaders make is to rush in and try to accomplish too much too quickly. Teachers return from their summer and discover that change has begun without them. Many leaders, administrators included, don't realize the danger associated with this approach because they are so focused on achieving their goals. When they do finally realize the danger, it is often too late. Even if no one publicly protests something you have implemented, the topic of conversation has already been set in the teachers' lunchroom: you will be perceived as an autocrat who has no intention of seeking their input, of treating them as professionals and equals.

For example, I know a leader who tried to separate the freshman class from the rest of the high school, in addition to sponsoring a weeklong activities fair that would encroach on classroom time. Although she had support from the administration, she did not have teacher support because she did not seek teacher input and rushed to make changes too soon. The results were disastrous: teachers had no buy-in, so they refused to support the proposals. Her credibility and reputation suffered, and the proposals soon died. So hold off on initiating or making major changes. If you're facing a dire situation, then some change can't be avoided, but refrain from making any moves that will be perceived as a complete program overhaul.

Invite Teachers to Participate in Change.

One of the first things that needed to be addressed when I was hired as chair was the curriculum. Jumping right into curriculum mapping would have been too much change too soon, so I decided to focus on the informal department policy of not having midterm examinations. Even though this would still mean implementing some modicum of change, it needed attention before the year started because midterms could be a valuable means of addressing lagging SOL scores.

The best way to ensure the success of this change, I believed, would be to learn how my teachers felt about the situation, how they thought we should go about implementing exams, and how they believed the assessments should look. Most important, I wanted them to construct the exams so that they would buy into them. I sent my future teachers an e-mail and a letter briefly explaining the need for midterms (that they can be more useful than final exams, which the department did have, because they yield information about areas needing remediation and can be used as teaching tools). A few teachers immediately responded positively, admitting that they had always thought the existing standard (or lack of one) was odd. They had never spoken up before because that was part of the culture and they didn't want to be seen as rocking the boat.

By inviting them in this manner rather than by "stating goals," as the teacher from the earlier scenario requested of me, I greatly reduced the possibility of being attacked for change. I secured curriculum pay for my teachers, and they came in over the summer to work on creating sample exams for each grade/subject level. Slightly more than half of the department chose to participate. The handful of summer meetings we had were extremely productive and a great team-building experience.

When everyone returned for inservice training at the beginning of the school year, the sample midterms were presented. Each person had the opportunity to refine the model exams at grade level team meetings. These teams were able to decide how they wanted to use the exams—as test banks, common assessments, or as indicators of the essential skills and knowledge that needed to be covered.

Afterward, the entire department reconvened to bring closure to our work. At that time, two or three teachers voiced their distress, claiming they had been deprived of the chance to give input during the creation of the exams. There was no need to defend myself. Those who had been present at the exams' conception— because they had devoted some of their summer and were now invested in this idea—quickly pointed out that everyone had been given the opportunity to participate in the project. And with that, we were able to move ahead, and four months later the entire department administered midterm exams.

The following summer, we worked on curriculum maps, and most teachers chose to participate in creating them. I then set aside three different dates and targeted those who chose not to participate to come in and meet with me to discuss the mapping, to review the maps, or to voice their concerns. A couple of teachers took advantage of this, which greatly reduced the amount of resistance toward the maps at our next inservice meeting.

Sell the Benefits, Not the Proposal.

I steered away from promoting the actual midterms and curriculum maps and instead focused on the benefits of having them. People are quick to buck against a program or an idea because they fear change; it is much harder to protest the benefits of something when they are clearly stated. The easiest way to sell the benefits of change is to explain that "this will help kids because . . ." or "this is good for students because . . ." Asking "Why do you think this is not good for students?" or "How will this not help kids?" or "How will this hurt students?" will help neutralize detractors. You will encounter teachers whose true motivation against a change is because it is not good for *them*, not because it's bad for students (and those who insist a change isn't good for students sometimes use that line of reasoning to hide their real motives). And some teachers tend to focus on personalities instead of programs, people instead of policies, which can immediately bias them against anything, so always try to bring the discussion back to how something will help students.

However, if you have a teacher who truly believes that the change does not best meet the needs of students, don't dismiss his point of view, especially in a group setting. If you do so, you will be seen as simply pulling rank. Think about how you would feel if an administrator said, "Because I said so," "Because I'm the principal," or "I have made an executive decision and it's not open to discussion." Exercising authority might make us feel good, but no one wants to follow a leader for those reasons.

Instead, it is necessary to encourage discussion with those who oppose change, although it might be time-consuming to do so. If they remain intransigent, approach them in a professional manner and ask them to show what they are basing their opposition on. Even if they have nothing, don't let that be the end of the matter.

You can still move ahead—especially because you do not need to have everyone behind an idea in order to move forward—but invite the opposition to continue looking for evidence in the meantime.

For example, one teacher vociferously expressed her objections, publicly and privately, about Sustained Silent Reading (SSR). She claimed that it didn't help students improve their reading comprehension. Most data indicate that reading scores improve when the program is implemented, but some researchers have charged that results are inconclusive. As much as I asked her to bring evidence for the department to review that demonstrated that SSR was harmful to students, she never did. If she had read something and had data to support her position, it would have become a valuable learning experience for both of us because a discussion could have sparked action research.

Turn resistance into unwitting cooperation.

Another alternative is to allow the teacher who continuously objects to serve as a control group. Data can then be analyzed and compared at the end of the year. Ultimately, the opposition will serve a purpose in the breach and will end up supporting the program.

Expect Disagreement (and Learn to Welcome It).

At times some of your teachers will be openly hostile toward you, and you may never come to understand why. If they publicly challenge you at a meeting, or use a meeting as a showcase to "speak daggers" to you, you should address the issues but not attack the people. You need to refrain from engaging in a quarrel.

One teacher spent most of a meeting muttering loudly enough that one side of the room could hear her say, "This is a waste of time. Why are we here?" and "What is *his* problem?" Teachers were so shocked by how brazen she was that they did not know how to react. Several people approached me after the meeting to express their displeasure with this teacher and their concerns about how this might affect the department's climate. Because other members had noticed this behavior, it was necessary for me to address it. I did so—but privately. After the next meeting, the same teachers commented that although her facial expressions showed her disdain, she kept her opinions to herself. They were pleased that a professional climate had been restored.

Because I had ignored her running commentary, I was perceived, as the cliché goes, as the bigger person. In fact, her behavior and my lack of response during the meeting galvanized support for me; if I had responded, I would have lost face for scolding a colleague or for demeaning her in front of peers. Sometimes this is a goal of recalcitrant teachers because it diminishes leadership. In such cases, the best defense is not to engage, which can annoy the detractors even more, especially the nicer you are.

Yet very few teachers are ill willed. When people base their opposition on the issues, that can be one of the best things for change. When people are critical about an idea, it causes us to examine it from different angles and dissect our position. They unknowingly help us build a stronger case by bringing to light other benefits or points of view of a proposal that we hadn't considered. And when you have gotten to know your teachers well, you will be able to anticipate and eliminate: you will be able to know what they will balk at or what and how they will argue, which will help you to better prepare how to sell or defend something. But you should also be flexible: it's OK if your idea is not exactly similar to what you originally proposed.

Defuse Threats.

We are all guilty of grumbling or making idle threats and saying things such as "this job isn't worth it" or "they can fire me now—just let them try to find someone to replace me." These comments help us vent our frustration with the bureaucracy that pervades the profession. They provide us some solace when we are forced outside of our comfort zone and help us cope when faced with our daily Herculean tasks. Of course, there will be those parent meetings that provoke such a visceral response. We may mean what we say at that moment; we may even have to bite back the tears. A week later the episode may still push us to the edge, but we realize that any decision made while our emotions are still raw would be a poor one: we are lucid enough to see that quitting would be disastrous.

But how do you handle these situations when you become a school leader, especially if you have teachers who really mean such threats? For example, you might have the kind of teacher who is married to a particular course till death do they part. When he learns that he will be teaching another class, he might respond with something along the lines of "I'll quit before I ever teach that course," "I paid my dues and I'm not working with those kids again—I'll put in for a transfer," or "but this course is my baby!" Such teachers might make threats—"Well, you can tell them that I'm going to resign" or "Make sure they know that there will be hell to pay"—with the expectation that you will pass them on to the administration because they are too afraid to do it themselves.

Never bring a threat—yours or someone else's—to the administration because you will never win (and even if it does work once for you, that will be the only time and you unknowingly may have done yourself more damage than good). Most administrators subscribe to the philosophy of "If they're not happy here, then they need to move on." It's that straightforward. Yet it sounds unfair. We are constantly reminded of the scarcity of quality teachers, so why would an administrator willingly let someone leave?

When I first encountered this attitude, I was taken aback: "She is one of my better teachers; how can we just let her go? I don't want to have to replace her!" But I soon discovered that I didn't enjoy being held hostage by the master schedule either, so I refused to succumb to threats. Quite simply, an administrator would rather take his chances with the applicant pool than continue working with someone who will make threats or become increasingly temperamental, recalcitrant, or intransigent no matter how talented she might be.

When teachers are so upset that they begin to "threaten with the threat," I tell them I don't feel comfortable bringing their position to the administration. I explain that although one of my roles as a leader is to support my team, it is suicide to go into a situation where the outcome is predetermined. However, I am quick to find some other way to show them that I support them. Sometimes it is as easy as merely recognizing that they feel strongly about something, not necessarily agreeing with them.

At one of my first department meetings, I was confronted with such a challenge. My teacher was dissatisfied with a teaming situation and I advised him against inappropriately vocalizing his frustrations. Making a threat is like drawing a gun: don't do it unless you're absolutely willing to squeeze the trigger. Even if you are ready and win the shootout, there are always consequences. I explained to my staff that we are all disposable, easily replaceable—including myself—so threats almost always backfire. This kind of talk endangered some people's egos and self-worth because in every building there are those who believe that the school would cease to exist if they were no longer around. The reality of teaching in a climate driven by high-stakes testing is that no one has the time or interest to coddle someone prone to histrionic fits.

One teacher was so offended by my response that he regularly brought it up during the next two years. When he discovered that he would not be teaching a class he had grown accustomed to teaching over the last five years, he was irate. Changing his schedule was not a ploy to edge him out; I didn't want him to leave, but the change was inevitable. He threatened to transfer, and the administration was not fazed. He believed that threatening to transfer was his trump card and that it would win the hand for him, but all it did was force the administration to walk away from the table. His plan backfired.

Of course, he could have stayed and taught his new schedule, but perhaps his pride had been wounded when he had overestimated his worth by believing he was going to get what he wanted. Or maybe he really did want to transfer. His decision forced me to spend an oppressive amount of time reviewing résumés and interviewing nearly everyone who applied to replace him. I wanted desperately to find an equally talented teacher and I did.

It is human nature to cling to the idea that the grass is always greener on the other side, which is why threats to transfer are so common. Think about how often you've heard teachers talk about a very supportive principal elsewhere they "just know" would be better, or about an administration that "actually listens" to its teachers, or a school where the parents are more involved. Yet as many teachers discover, schools are schools, and students are students. Even if some things are better elsewhere, there are still problems that irk the faculty. No matter how strong the leadership or morale or test scores, there is no perfect school. Be quick to remind teachers of this when they're on the verge of threatening to leave if they don't get what they want.

Defusing a threat or limiting the number of meetings the administration has with your teachers is crucial: if you don't limit the amount of static that makes its way to the main office, it will reflect on your department—and on your leadership. It's understandable that situations will need to be brought to an administrator from time to time. However, administrators can be quick to label teachers as high maintenance or as prima donnas, especially if their interaction with them centers on dealing with a crisis (or, more accurately, a perceived crisis). Administrators will begin to tune out all their concerns, even if you are present, and even if it is important. These teachers will be viewed as a time-consuming drain on resources. As a result, administrators may no longer hold that teacher in the same regard that you do, which could cause them to lose confidence in your judgment.

To avoid such problems, it is essential to learn early on what issues are most significant to your teachers. When you first assume your leadership position, ask teachers during inservice week what their greatest concerns are about the school, their greatest peeves about the system. This will help you to better read crises as the year develops, enabling you to determine which situations are a "must handle."

Don't Let the Same Dog Bite You Twice.

When I was five years old, my friend's dog bit my cousin on the wrist without provocation. At that young age, my cousin learned to negotiate an uneasy truce with the dog. We can learn from the wisdom of children. If a staff member "bites" you, then don't let it happen a second time.

Sometimes we need to have these situations pointed out to us. After complaining to an administrator about a recurring situation with a teacher, he responded, "What do you expect when you keep handing him the knife?" In other situations, it can be a case of knowing when to walk away. It's human nature to fight back, to survive, to protect oneself, but sometimes the best thing to do is learn how to avoid a bad situation in the first place. Just as the young boy above learned to avoid the dog, you too need to develop some kind of truce so that you are not constantly fighting the same battles and expending your energy by chasing your tail. To gain better footing, determine what the person is really after, what he really values, and what his true intentions are.

Build Support by Identifying Your Supporters.

The politics of change require that you politick for change. For change or your leadership to be successful, it is necessary to devote a good deal of time to working the network of teachers, counselors, administrators, and parents. Bounce ideas off your teachers during lunch or after school to see how they feel. Before initiating, announcing, or supporting a change, talk to your teachers informally and let them do PR work for you by selling the benefits to other teachers. In order to achieve change, coalition building is often necessary. But this is a dangerous area because you don't want to be perceived as biasing people or as creating factions or a rift in your team.

Let Someone Else Propose the Change.

Because of data on Sustained Silent Reading, I strongly believed that implementing an SSR program departmentwide would be one of the keys to improving our reading scores. However, I was aware that too much change might make teachers uncomfortable and that some would oppose what I was suggesting simply because it came from me. Early in the school year, I discovered that my reading teacher was a proponent of SSR. I explained to her that I would be presenting some reading strategies at a department meeting, and I asked if she would be willing to speak on SSR.

She agreed, and her enthusiasm during the presentation was contagious. By the end of the meeting, in addition to wanting more reading strategies, teachers wanted more information about the program from her. At the following month's meeting, teachers were saying that "we really should be doing this in our school" and "the kids would really go for this." A groundswell had taken shape, and by the next meeting, the department was nearly unanimous in thinking that we should start an SSR program.

The program was (and still is) a success. The irony is that this might not have been the outcome if I had proposed it. Because it was a teacher—not I—who recommended the idea (which began as staff development), and because we carefully examined the suggestion rather than rushing into anything, the department didn't feel forced into the program. Some leaders make the mistake of wanting to get the credit for a successful idea. Abandon this mentality. You'll earn far more credit and credibility from your teachers for being hands-off while facilitating change (besides, if test scores do improve, you'll ultimately get some credit for that anyway).

Be Involved, Not Hands-On.

Being hands-on connotes control and meddling, whereas being involved implies knowing what is going on but not always taking over or taking control. An involved leader is comfortable with delegating responsibility, but a hands-on leader would never consider that. An involved leader is aware of his teachers' important dates and deadlines. He does not necessarily rush in to take over a situation but makes sure that he is available when needed as a resource.

Instead of being overly controlling, focus on building your teachers' respect for you by being available and accessible. Weaker teachers might need you more, but don't ignore your all-stars because you assume that they and their kids will be all right. If you overlook them, they might become hostile to your leadership. Although it's natural to want others to see you as being in charge, if you present yourself as a hands-on leader, you will have a tough time convincing them to follow your leadership and respect your authority.

Come to Consensus.

Derived from "consent," which means to give permission or to agree, consensus is often viewed as an attractive alternative to voting. Much educational literature emphasizes achieving consensus, but what some advocates seem to ignore is that gaining consensus is not always easy nor is it a neat process. Trying to delve beneath people's positions to reveal their motives behind roadblocking can be tedious. You may never discover their true reasons, and these people may never be persuaded that what is on the floor is the best solution.

Even though consensus building can be ripe with conflict, a straight vote can create a more adversarial atmosphere. What consensus building allows for is dialogue and negotiation in an attempt to move forward. As I mentioned earlier, by using the fist-five technique in drafting a departmental mission statement, everyone had some kind of input in its adoption, and we were able to create a statement that everyone could live with. Although that does not sound especially noble, sometimes the best you can hope for is to come up with something that everyone is willing to live with or adhere to.

It bears repeating that one of the problems with consensus building is the recent wave of "valuing the contributions" of all people. It sounds warm and fuzzy on the surface, and although there is nothing inherently wrong with this philosophy, it creates value relativism—no matter what one says, it is deemed important because it came from a professional. But what if people offer trite or worthless suggestions? What if someone is blatantly incorrect? True, we need to learn how to work with one another and come to agreement, but worrying more about an adult's self-esteem is ultimately damaging to children. Keep in mind that you can value someone's contribution simply by seeking feedback, but you don't have to incorporate it just because it was made. Finally, there is a time and place for consensus. As much as people want to be involved in decision making, not all decisions can or should be arrived at through this process.

Don't Blame Someone Else.

Your teachers need to know that your motives are honest. If they suspect that you are conducting research, they will be unwilling to try (or they will derail) new ideas. Similarly, if you are going to implement something new, don't blame someone else for the idea. A leader I knew would publicly blame her administrators for any new proposal, whether it came from them or not. Depending on the situation, this either riles people against the administration or causes them to doubt their leader. It is critical to avoid this culture of blame. Your teachers will never have buy-in when you are passing the buck.

Additionally, they may take you at your word and confront the administration over what you told them. If you announce your displeasure with the administration's decision by publicly stating at a meeting that "this too shall pass," you will be telling your team that you are not taking a decision seriously, and neither should they. Worst of all, if one of your teachers is then accused of sabotaging an administrative decision, in the end the teacher will blame you. When it gets too hot in the kitchen, people do not always automatically look for the exit—sometimes they first find someone else to throw into the fire.

Know Where the Emergency Exits Are.

Before entering into any kind of meeting with a teacher (or a group of teachers) that you believe could be problematic, you need to have both an entry and an exit strategy. How will you open the discussion—will you state your opinion first or listen to the teacher's viewpoint first? Weigh the gravity of the situation and set a time limit on your discussion (and let your teacher know what it will be, which will help you stay focused on the issue and avoid covering old ground).

If the end of the meeting or conference is quickly approaching, don't succumb to the pressure of making a decision. It is acceptable to end a meeting without a (re)solution as long as it is clear to all parties that you will resume the discussion at some point in the near future and that the lack of an outcome does not signify that you have acquiesced or approved something. Some leaders have a tendency to think, especially when working with a larger group, that they must always find a resolution because that is what leaders do: they make decisions or facilitate decision making. Instead, use the interim to continue brainstorming or researching the issue. Although a defining characteristic of good leadership and teaching is decisiveness, if someone pushes and presses you for a decision, then he may be trying to take advantage of the situation.

A leader should never make—and is more likely to regret— a rushed decision.

Sometimes withholding a solution can be another valuable exit strategy. Allow everyone to brainstorm and discuss solutions, and when it seems that the team is weary or frustrated by the process, and eager to have closure, then present a solution. Your team will be more open to your solution if they have exhausted all other avenues, and by presenting it at the end of a meeting, they will not feel that you steamrolled the decision-making process. Also, in terms of an exit strategy, have a trump card ready, something that you are confident will tip the balance in your favor (but make sure it is professional).

Focus on Containing, Not on Winning.

A parent sometimes gives her children something to do while she prepares dinner so that she can get done what she needs to get done. One colleague espouses handling obstacles on a team the same way. Because it is very difficult to win over or overcome those who oppose you, instead focus on containing them. For example, with the SSR situation, I knew that the teacher who objected to the program was not going to acquiesce or transfer to another school. If she had taken my advice and researched articles to support her view, she might have become preoccupied with the endeavor, leaving her little time to challenge other issues. The busier people are, the less likely that they will find the time to oppose you.

Pull the Train out of the Station.

In both our professional and social lives, we commonly use a train as a metaphor to express how we feel about something or to relay how something went. We say things such as "he derailed the entire meeting," "we really need to get back on track," or "what a train wreck that idea was." Similarly, when implementing change, consider another train metaphor. Again, you will rarely have complete agreement, but when you get a strong majority of people behind you, it's time to pull the train out of the station. You've done all you can do to persuade them about the benefits of a proposal and about the need for a program, and they've heard the train starting up. To board or not to board is their choice. They can stamp their feet on the platform in disagreement with which direction the train is heading but that will not prevent it from leaving the station nor will it bring it back. The best they can hope for is catching up with the train at the next stop. And if most everyone else is on board, they probably don't want to be the only ones still standing at the station.

Ostensibly, it sounds harsh to ostracize someone, but sometimes the best way to motivate someone is to move him, or push him, outside of his comfort zone. Most people want to be a part of the pack. They desire to be accepted and will go along with the program because that can lead to acceptance. If they choose not to join up, isolation is not necessarily a bad thing; it can work to your advantage because it can neutralize people, even if only temporarily. Turnover is not merely acceptable when it comes to change, it is sometimes desirable as well as unavoidable. If the person chooses to stay, he may grudgingly board the train, but he might attempt to derail it (or even hijack it) in the future. At that point, however, you should already have momentum on your side.

Although it takes several people for a train to run smoothly, there can ultimately be just one engineer, one person who drives the train. As the leader, you are that person: you have the right to pull the train out of the station. Who better than you knows when people are onboard and ready to depart? As the engineer, you have the best view of the tracks ahead and the best knowledge of how fast you should be moving. This also goes for working with your administrators. They may have more experience or a better understanding of the big picture, but you know your teachers best and you know best what is needed to improve your program. Even so, don't ignore the warning signs and signals that may pop up along the way that indicate you need to slow down or refuel.

Mediating Conflicts

As I have outlined, one of your responsibilities as a teacher leader is conflict resolution, handling and overcoming problematic situations that arise in your department. There are, however, other yet similar scenarios that will demand your involvement if you wish to maintain a healthy, productive environment. The difficulty is that these situations extend outside of your department: they include other teachers.

With an apparent increase in the number of teamed classes in master schedules across the United States, the likelihood increases that you will need to serve as mediator between one of your teachers and a teacher from another department. For example, one of your teachers might be teamed with a special education teacher when there are a certain number of students with learning disabilities in the class. Such teamed classes can be challenging because the special education teacher is not directly under your leadership even though she works closely with your teachers. You need to be perceived as supportive of your teacher yet simultaneously neutral if there is a dispute.

A teamed situation is like a marriage: there will be personality conflicts, philosophical disagreements, and clashes over how to best rear the children. Divorce is rarely an option, so a poor teaming environment left unattended can be catastrophic. A weak teaming situation breeds mistrust and miscommunication, turns professionals petty, makes teachers resent their jobs and their students, and eventually causes teachers to leave the school. With shared teaching, planning, grading, federal mandates, and student success at stake, teaming can indeed be a volatile situation.

Too often, teamed teachers put off discussing problems with their counterparts because they fear that dialogue will be perceived as confrontation, suggestions as attacks. Teachers need to understand that a discussion about the state of their classroom with their partner—and partner is an important word here because both should have equal ownership of the classroom—might become confrontational, but such a conversation is a professional responsibility.

Sometimes teachers believe the situation will improve on its own, so perhaps it is best to ignore it. As in personal relationships, situations rarely resolve themselves when ignored. Like the husband and wife who delay counseling until the final stages of their marriage, a teacher who brings issues to you midway through the year diminishes the chances of reconciliation. Stress to your teachers that they need to be open with their team teachers and not procrastinate when they believe a discussion about their class is necessary. Encourage teachers to immediately bring to your attention any problems, no matter how small, to prevent them from escalating and to increase the chance of resolution. This allows you to give advice and prevents you from being blindsided down the road. You won't be able to fix every problem or mend every relationship, but perhaps you will at least be able to make a teamed class bearable for the parties involved, which will ultimately help the students and have a positive effect on both the core and the special education departments.

Just Listen.

Even if you have an idea of who is in the right and who is in the wrong, the worst thing you can do is to immediately cast judgment. As a marriage counselor will do early on in a session, just listen. Don't judge right off the bat. Sometimes the teachers might simply need someone to hear them vent. Observe how they interact, which can give you an idea of what is really the problem. Does one cut the other off? Is one more aggressive than the other? Listen to what each of them believes to be the problem. Is it a question of content knowledge? Does one believe that he is always the "bad guy" in the classroom? Is someone not making himself available to plan? Are individualized education programs not being followed? Gather as much information as you can before actively involving yourself in the conference. In addition, make the environment conducive to dialogue. Meet in neutral territory (not one of their rooms), set up chairs so that the teachers can face each other, and make sure that there are no desks or tables, which can be seen as barriers, in between them.

"Let Me Make an Observation."

Once you do become actively involved in the meeting, you should behave like a mediator, not an arbiter. It would be disastrous if you were perceived as favoring one teacher over the other. You are not there to take sides, to point out who is wrong and who is right, nor to punish anyone. Leave that for the administrators. Instead, your role is to facilitate the dialogue, to enhance growth. Ask penetrating questions. Clarify and summarize what has been stated. Paraphrase what one has said so that the other is clear about the issue at hand.

When you do feel it is necessary to make some kind of judgment, couch your views in the following terms: "If I can make an observation here . . . ," "What I am observing is . . . ," "From what has been said, it seems that . . ." Never allow yourself to be perceived as stating an absolute. Avoid at all costs conclusive and definitive phrases and make sure that everything you are saying is an observation or a perception—an observation is open to debate because you're not claiming to be the authority or expert. "You are negative," "You aren't pulling your weight," or "You just don't know your content matter" are phrases that will put a teacher on the defensive and cause her to challenge you. Tread carefully because, as in all cases, the language that you choose is critical and will have a direct bearing on how the rest of the meeting progresses and on its outcome.

To better cover yourself, be sure to have the other department chair present. Because you don't want to be perceived as taking sides, having the other chair present will show that the two of you are seeking answers and trying to help your teachers come up with answers.

Clarify Roles, Set Goals.

When mediating between a special education teacher and a core teacher, you will discover that one of the main impediments to success is that the teachers are unclear of their roles and often uncomfortable expressing this. If a teacher has never teamed before, he might be uncomfortable with someone sharing his room and unsure of how much control of his class he needs to relinquish. Or perhaps, because teachers can be territorial, he is uncomfortable sharing space with someone new. In other cases, a core teacher who has teamed with someone for years now finds himself having to team with someone new. This can be unsettling and can result in a tumultuous situation if he clings to the same expectations he had with his previous team teacher.

Similarly, a team teacher might have difficulty understanding how she fits in with a new routine. She might feel slighted as a professional because she is not being given enough responsibility, believing her role has been reduced to that of an aide. Or she might feel overwhelmed because she thinks too much is being asked of her. In a more extreme scenario, one teacher—or both—might believe the team is being hindered by incompetence.

There are no easy solutions to such obstacles, but a good starting point is to help the teachers define their roles. Ask both teachers to state or write down (prior to or during the meeting) what they believe their partner's role should be (Resource 17). This technique will yield useful information about the state of the team and can facilitate setting boundaries and expectations. By the end of the meeting, try to have the team teachers come to some kind of understanding or agreement about their roles and responsibilities, about how much or how little each expects of the other. Set goals, document them, and follow up in a month to check on progress and to see what, if any, tweaking is needed (Resource 18).

"Are You Comfortable with That?"

When setting goals and determining how to improve a teamed situation, don't ask the teachers if they agree with a proposal. This closes the door on the proposal because it leaves little room for further discussion. You won't always be able to get each teacher to agree on something, so what you might be looking for is a compromise. By asking teachers if they are comfortable with what is on the table, you are allowing for a negotiation and potentially avoiding someone shutting down. And by using such a statement, you're not asking if they agree with something—you're asking to what level or extent they can live with it, which might be the best that you can hope for.

Match People Up.

Many teaming problems can be avoided by ensuring that teachers are teamed with their best possible match. These matches can be based on the totality of personality, philosophy, and work ethic, or on just one of these elements. Or in the same way you might pair up a shy student and a gregarious student or a weak student and a strong student, consider what makes the best team.

Knowing your teachers can help you match them up, but you should consider other means as well. A few weeks prior to master scheduling, the special education chair in my school organized what I like to call a "speed dating session." During a lunch hour where pizza was provided (to help ensure attendance), teachers had 30 minutes to meet, talk, and eat with potential team teachers so they could get a better idea of whom they thought they best matched up with. And when master scheduling was slated for discussion at a department meeting, I would distribute "wish lists" to my teachers to determine who was open to teaming and who wanted to team with whom.

Develop a Rapport with the LD Chair.

Of all the people you need to develop a professional relationship with, the chair of the special education department can be one of the most important because of the scenarios presented at the beginning of this section. Develop a relationship with this person based on trust so that you can bring information about a teamed class to her without your teachers feeling as if they have been sold out. This team leader or department chair is a vital resource and she will be able to help you brainstorm solutions and assist when mediation is necessary. Such a partnership will benefit your students and your instructional program.

5

Motivational Leadership

Building Climate and Community

The holidays are sharp reminders of just how little society values educators. Even though we may be comfortable with our salaries and the fact that we will never be wealthy, when we hear friends or relatives bragging about a Christmas bonus or bemoaning a smaller than normal year-end bonus, it is difficult to sympathize: no such rewards system exists in schools. If we're lucky, we receive highlighters or pens or some other trinkets. If we stay in one district for a few years, we may receive a pin recognizing our service.

I am not belittling such tokens because they do serve a useful function: they make us feel appreciated. We may grumble about the school magnet we received in our in-box as a holiday gift, because we sometimes feel so dehumanized and devalued, but we are grateful that someone noticed us or realized that we are committed to pushing the organization ahead despite the bumps along the way.

Oftentimes, our main need is for our supervisors to demonstrate that they are paying attention. Recently, one of my teachers was named the lead mentor in the school, so she had the responsibility of creating an inservice program for all the new hires. When I called her that afternoon to see how it had gone, before our conversation ended, she said, "Thanks so much for paying attention and knowing that it was today!" A pick-me-up or a kind word can often solve much of what upsets us professionally. Perhaps your teachers are experiencing a rough stretch because of taxing parent conferences or are scrambling to finish grading 120 research papers, and they just need you to acknowledge this.

In more serious cases, the overall climate needs an injection of professionalism grounded in sympathy and compassion. When I began as English chair, the balkanization present in the department had fomented gossip, jealousy, and pettiness. There was little sense of teamwork, camaraderie, and willingness to share. People were isolated, and they resented those who were creating a negative atmosphere: poison had seeped into the well.

I don't believe empirical evidence is really needed to tell us that when morale goes down, not only do we suffer as professionals *and* as people, but our students are adversely affected as well. It is imperative to reduce this kind of atmosphere and cultivate community in order to improve performance and production. There are several easy ways—some professional, some social, and some that overlap—to create a positive climate and environment, to recognize and support your teachers, and to keep morale high.

Promoting a Professional Climate

Even though we are all professionals in that we are engaged in a field that requires specialized knowledge, this does not mean that all teams or leaders foster a professional atmosphere. Of course, adhering to ethical standards and treating colleagues fairly, honestly, and respectfully stimulates such a climate, but there are other elements that can enrich it. You cannot take for granted that the climate on your team or in your building will be professional: you need to ensure this by actively creating, nurturing, and promoting a supportive environment.

Conduct a Walk-Through.

Although some teachers cringe when an administrator walks into their classrooms, many more would welcome visits to show the many good things that go on in their rooms. I have talked with teachers who appear to be relieved that they weren't observed, but paradoxically these same people also expressed frustration that an administrator was unable to find time to visit their classes. Teachers want someone to recognize a great activity or lesson. They want to be noticed.

Rather than spending 30 to 40 minutes observing a teacher, I will sometimes perform a walk-through instead. Armed with yellow sticky notes, I sit in a class for a maximum of 10 minutes. This enables me to visit several rooms during my planning period without completely consuming my time. If the students are engaged in an activity, I circulate around the room and talk with them about what they are doing. On my way out, I'll stick a note on the teacher's chair, lectern, or desk with a brief, positive message: "What a great activity! I love how you're using learning stations," "The kids were really engaged in an insightful discussion centering on challenging ideas," or "Your explanation of scansion would have helped me when I was in school," and "I wish I could stay longer!"

You can also perform a variation on the walk-through. Think about how exciting it is to find a note on the bathroom mirror from a loved one when you don't expect it. You can do something similar. Stand unobtrusively outside of the classroom and note what is going on, or speak with a student in the hall and then leave a note later in your teacher's room as a surprise, telling her how much a student enjoyed a particular discussion or how deftly she handled the interruption of the fire drill.

Everyone loves positive feedback, and many teachers crave being evaluated just like their students do. Make your feedback as specific as possible (much as you would with your students) because statements such as "nice work" or "great job" are not powerful or necessarily motivating, and they can smack of insincerity. Your students can sense patronizing and insincerity, and your teachers will too, so don't force a comment solely for the sake of making one. Instead, recognize teachers doing something at their best (don't use this as an opportunity to find shortcomings). Maybe they had a great activity or an extremely productive collaboration session with a colleague, or successfully mediated a disagreement between two teachers.

If you don't find something right away, invest the time. It's worth it. If you know your teachers well, most of the time you should be able to find something fairly easily. But be sure that your praise relates to their performance. Although we all enjoy a compliment on a new haircut or a new outfit, this kind of praise does not boost morale or improve performance.

Keep Your Finger on the Pulse.

A few times a week, at the beginning and end of the day, I try to stop into different teachers' rooms to see how they are doing. Consequently, I sometimes find out about situations, concerns, or issues that my teachers might not bring to me because they are so busy. These impromptu visits save them some time; it also shows that I care. It can be as easy as popping your head in their doors after school and asking, "How was your day?" If I discover that a teacher has had a particularly trying day, I give him time to clear his head and follow up with a phone call in the evening to determine if he is still upset and how important the issue is to him. If you create such a compassionate climate, and avoid being intrusive, you'll find your teachers will emulate this behavior.

Support Your Team.

Obviously, you want to support your teachers. Regardless of what current educational reform is in favor, teachers are still alone in their rooms five days a week. Even if you have implemented teams and created a professional atmosphere, teachers can ultimately feel alone because of the singular nature of the job. They need to feel supported; they need to believe that they are supported. Let them know that they are not in it alone, that you have their back. You need to show no fear (if something needs to be brought to the administration) in order for them to have faith in you and the chain of command.

Of course, there will certainly be times when you will be unable to provide support—perhaps you have a better understanding of the bigger picture or you already know the outcome. The teachers' first instinct, though, should be that you are going to support them. And supporting them does not necessarily mean always agreeing with them. They might know that they're in the wrong, but they will still feel supported if the culture you create is not one of pointing out faults and assigning blame. Instead, ask what they have learned from the experience and then discuss it. Sometimes support can be as simple as saying, "I understand."

A climate of trust and respect must be established and nurtured.

To better support a teacher in instructional matters, prior to mediating a parent conference or similar meeting, take the time to determine what previous proactive measures she has taken, what she expects will happen at the conference, or if she needs to tell you anything before the conference begins. Explain to her beforehand that you will have the parent speak first (because sometimes parents only need to vent), so that she won't perceive your actions as a lack of support. Meeting with your teacher first to explain your course of action will allow her to vent (because sometimes that is all that teachers need) as you play counselor. This can reduce the chances of her going into the meeting on the offensive.

You may find that you will also need to support teachers in their personal affairs. Perhaps it is a relationship gone sour, a family situation boiling over, or a car problem causing frustration—the point is that they may seek you out. If they don't, it's still a good idea to check in on them if you hear something through the grapevine. Talking with your teachers about personal matters can be a way to show your support, especially if *you* are willing to open up and demonstrate vulnerability, that you are human too. Listen to them even if it is about something that you think is trivial; the minor things tend to take their toll and gnaw away at our desire to achieve.

However, you should use caution on how involved you become in these matters. A colleague once expressed her frustration to me that out of the blue her chair asked her, "Are you Catholic? You know that yesterday was a day of obligation, right?" This kind of conversation is not inherently bad, but if it is unprovoked or makes the teacher feel uncomfortable, then it crosses the line.

Look for other opportunities to support your teachers, such as when they want to try something new. Maybe they are starting a new activity or trying an alternative assessment and need some supplies from you. Find a way to get them what they need. Maybe they want to implement a new instructional strategy. Locate pertinent research or literature for them (and when you do, follow up by discussing the article and their experiences). Support them even when it is unrelated to instruction. Someone might propose a "Hawaiian shirt Friday," and even if you just know that this will not catch on, buy yourself a Hawaiian shirt for that day. If only one or two people wear one, or if some snicker, most will privately respect you for putting yourself out there. And that is half the battle—earning their respect.

But probably the most significant way you can help is by supporting teachers in the high-stakes culture of No Child Left Behind and grade analysis. If test scores or quarter grades come in lower than expected and you know your teachers have done all that they can do, then collect supporting evidence and sing their praises from the mountaintop. Unfortunately, judging from the reaction of most administrators and politicians, and from reading current educational literature, the present undertones imply that there is always a way to make every child a genius. Best practices, child study testing, and collaboration are valuable methods to helping students achieve, but sometimes the painful truth, the truth that we are afraid to whisper, is that some students may have achieved all that they can achieve. (And another truth is that we are becoming more interested in rewarding effort over productivity.)

Just because some students are earning *D*s does not mean that your teachers have not tried every possible way to improve their instruction and to enhance learning. Perhaps your teachers do not deserve to be persecuted by the administration and parents. We can't turn every outfielder into a Joe DiMaggio, regardless of what some may claim and regardless of how hard some might try. To assume that all students can be successful to the same degree or at the same rate is foolish rhetoric. For example, if a student takes a physical education course, that does not mean he is ready, or ever will be ready, to start on a varsity team. Therefore, your job as a leader is to support your teachers if they find themselves in a politically incorrect position of having students who are not achieving.

Inquire about their test analysis, data, assessments, and remediation strategies and determine if they are valid. If everything that can and should be done is being done, then let the administration and parents know that the student is receiving what she needs. Document that the teacher is providing the skills and knowledge to at least bring the student up to grade level rather than manipulating averages to avoid the accusation of low grades or to satisfy some bureaucratic mandate.

Cultivating Community

Creating or advancing a professional climate is just one aspect of having a proficient and productive team. Because teachers spend so much of their time isolated, working individually, or even going the entire day without talking with other adults, you need to bring your teachers together. Establishing a sense of connection, belonging, interdependence, and growth will make a group more cohesive and develop community, another factor essential to your success as a leader and their efficacy as a team.

Engage in Team Building.

Administrators who state, "Because you are professionals, you'll be able to work together," or who believe that departments will be effective because they are expected to be, miss the point entirely. They either don't understand human nature or choose to ignore its shortcomings. Don't make that mistake. Just as some classes engage in team-building activities in the beginning of the year to foster community, it is essential that you implement team-building and trust-building activities.

For example, before one of my inservice meetings at the beginning of the year, I brought in a set of baseball cards. After each teacher received a card, we stepped into the hall so teachers could find out who had the card with the matching team. This allowed them to talk for a short while upon returning to school, but more important, it organized them into pairs and prevented them from gravitating only toward their friends. Each pair then had to decide who would be the "leader" and who would be the "follower." Imitating an innocuous fraternity trust-building activity, each pair entered the room with the leader guiding his partner, who had his eyes closed. Once everyone had sat down, we briefly discussed how each pair went about navigating a way to the seats (some teachers had already begun talking about this while watching from the hallway).

I commented on how people had trusted their partners to lead them safely to their seats: if we could trust one another to do that, then we should be able to trust one another to do the right thing, to do what needs to be done. We then discussed how some walked backward to lead their followers into the room, guiding them by their voices; others indicated what kind of turn was needed and how many degrees to move; and still others gave explicit directions on how many steps were needed at every turn. Our discussion culminated by affirming the various ways that people chose to get from point A to point C, a metaphor for how we should function as a department: embracing diverse thinking and trusting that our colleagues will help us as we journey toward a common goal.

Nurture Growth and Professionalism.

Collaboration and cooperation is critical for success, both personal and standardized. We confer with friends and family before making a life-changing decision or even a minor one, so why wouldn't we do the same when it comes to kids?

When most of us began our first year of teaching, we inherited classes and subject matter we were unfamiliar with ("No one ever taught me how to teach *Hamlet*," "We never discussed how to make science meaningful to students' lives," and the like). Weighed down with perhaps the most challenging teaching load in the school ("You need to pay your dues," "Because they have seniority") and handicapped by being asked to serve on almost every committee in addition to sponsoring an activity or two, we barely kept our heads above water. Most do not. We researched ways to turn what might be a flat lecture into an engaging activity (pre-Internet, mind you) and functioned on four hours of sleep as we toiled all night to create a challenging yet fair test (and a make-up one in anticipation of absenteeism). Some of our senior colleagues shared ideas and lessons while others refused to share because they felt that we "had to learn to either sink or swim."

Whether you have novice teachers or an experienced team, sharing ideas, strategies, and lessons is important not just because it is good for kids, but because it is good for us. At the very least, it makes an unwieldy job more manageable. We find out more about education and learning by discussing our experiences with colleagues. We grow by learning from experience, as much from others' as from our own.

Collaborators evolve into learning partners, equally invested in each other and in improving achievement.

Student teachers are often grouped into cohorts required to meet on a regular basis to debrief, discuss, and devise successful strategies. So, from the onset, teachers are expected to work with and learn from one another. But when most teachers take their first job, they discover that this is not the norm in the building, that the culture is one of isolation and not one of collaboration. As a result, most conform to this culture, thereby perpetuating it.

Demonstrate transformational leadership by changing the culture of your team, which can also influence teams throughout the building. First, make an effort to support the sharing of ideas, strategies, and lessons. You might try setting up a central filing cabinet to house materials to be shared. Find a way to offer ideas without being overbearing. My building's technology specialist was able to create server space for each of my grade level teams so they could trade ideas, post PowerPoint presentations, or download test items.

Once people have begun to share, the next logical step is to talk about what they have shared. Even if you chair an elective or a subject where there are many "singletons," which would seemingly preclude such professional dialogues, at the most basic level your teachers should be able to collaborate and grow as professionals because they all are responsible for planning, assessing, and, quite simply, being in a classroom. Hold a meeting for teachers of singletons to brainstorm areas they have in common. At the very least, they should be able to compare classroom management, how they handle attendance (do they have specific procedures in place for monitoring student attendance?), and the like, so they can indeed learn from one another. These teachers can also talk about instruction. As a colleague once noted, best practices don't change from discipline to discipline. Teachers can search their subject matter for common areas such as reading and understanding directions, note-taking and study skills, and so on.

The downside to collaboration—in addition to teacher resistance from those who feel uncomfortable with the concept and prefer working alone, are suspicious of others, or are frustrated by their colleagues—is that some leaders try to force it because they see it as a seemingly easy fix or as a panacea to improving achievement. What they fail to realize is that an initial level of trust needs to be established. So don't rush this process. It is only when we are comfortable with our vulnerability, or no longer feel vulnerable, that we are more willing to work together. Just as you should be open to the idea of having your teachers evaluate your leadership, you should encourage your teachers to assess how well they meet or work as teams (Resource 19).

Yet collaboration should be more than working together on lessons, activities, or data analysis. On some of the grade level teams in my department, teachers routinely gather for "blind assessments." They read essays where, instead of their names, students have used identification numbers or some other code name to ensure a fair process. After agreeing on the rubric and anchor papers, teachers circulate the papers so that each has had a chance to read and score them, and then they discuss the results. In other instances, some upper grade level teachers score underclass essays so that students are aware of future expectations. This also gives these teachers a better idea of what problem areas they will be inheriting in the future, which gives them time to start thinking about adjusting curriculum maps and lessons.

One final example of collaboration, a unique one at that, involves classroom management. When a teacher is having problems with a student who is either not producing or is being difficult in class, she speaks with the student's previous teacher, or with one he had a connection with. In many cases, these teachers talk privately with the student to determine what is going on and what can be done to remedy the situation, and they work with each other to find solutions. In more extreme situations, one of my teachers has not hesitated to ask another teacher to come into a class to assist with classroom management—not because he is weak in this area, but because of the class size and class composition—which ultimately reduced disruptions and allowed the teacher to devote more individualized attention.

This kind of collaboration even extends into our English department hallway, where teachers ensure that students are behaving properly and following the rules not only by being visible outside their doorways but by walking and talking among the kids in between classes. At the end of the second year of this practice, students dreaded encountering an English teacher, especially a former one, more than running into their own administrator! Working together in this fashion helped us to improve our learning environment and showed students that we were serious about what we did and that they should be as well. Collaboration can take a variety of forms, but what remains the same is that it is a vital component to the well-being of a school.

Emphasize Staff Development.

Provide meaningful professional development tailored to department needs as well as to individual needs. One of the defining characteristics of teachers is our curiosity and our desire to learn. Feed this hunger and keep teachers coming back to the buffet by making professional development the culture, not something simply and solely done to satisfy bureaucratic mandates.

Have your teachers gather to learn rather than to listen to you. In collaboration with your team, analyze data to ascertain apparent weaknesses in your program and create staff development to remedy them. For example, ask teachers to bring copies of a successful lesson, activity, or assessment to a meeting for the team to discuss. Or have teachers present a mini-lesson, activity, or assessment that targets specific growth areas, objectives, or learning strands. Provide professional literature for your teachers to review at a meeting or the next meeting, or suggest they read articles on their own and report back to the group. You might even consider starting a professional library for your team by purchasing or obtaining books related to your discipline. As another learning opportunity, encourage your teachers to join professional organizations and attend conferences, and set aside meeting time for them to share their experiences. Then, at the end of meetings, use exit slips similar to ones you would use in your classroom to ask teachers what they still have questions about, what they want to know more about, and what they are willing to present about in the future. These techniques could set your agenda for the entire year. When topics and presentations come from your team, rather than from you, it automatically creates more buy-in and interest in meetings.

But staff development does not always need to be a formal, carefully planned program. Informal staff development can occur during lunch, or wherever and whenever teachers are gathered. There will be times when gossip or complaints dominate the lunchroom conversation, but eventually teachers will talk about what they are doing in their classrooms. It is in our blood. Whether we like to brag, want validation, or are eager to share, lunch talk can often come back to teaching. If other topics reign, try to subtly steer the conversation by asking someone what she is presently teaching or by sharing how your class is going. Such talk does not need to occur every day, but you should try to capitalize on moments when teachers are together.

Encourage Reflection.

Team members should be committed to becoming better teachers, and the first step in that direction is reflecting on what we do and how we do it. Without reflection, we cannot refine what we do. When we reflect on an activity or a lesson, whether it is between classes, over a day, or during the summer, we are proud for noticing and making the necessary changes in both unsuccessful and successful lessons. This renews us. It refreshes us and gives us the energy and interest to introduce our new and improved product.

When there is no meaningful professional development, or teachers don't reflect on their practices, they stagnate or they stunt their own growth. Their zeal for the job dulls and they only go through the motions. Think of the history teacher whom your older brother had, your friends had, and you had, and all of you took the exact same tests and completed the exact same activities. Are teachers truly doing right by students when this happens? Encourage your teachers to reflect on their practices privately, in conferences, or at team meetings. It is only when we reflect and are honest with ourselves that we grow as professionals and as people.

If we don't grow, or are unwilling to grow, how can we expect our students to push themselves, to try new things, and to grow? Once teachers reflect on their practices and you provide time and guidance to refine practices, you have helped them renew themselves. When a teacher feels renewed, the energy, excitement, and enthusiasm is palpable and contagious among both students and teachers, which can have a positive effect on student achievement.

Whereas teachers can view themselves, their classroom personas, and their lessons one way, their students may see them in a completely different light. The same holds true for you as a leader in how you view yourself, your leadership, and your team. Have your teachers reflect on and discuss what kind of department they are a part of, what its strengths and weaknesses are. This dialogue can be similar to when you create a mission statement, and it serves as a good self-check. You can also create a survey for your department or team so that you can assess and reflect on your leadership and determine how you can better serve your teachers and what group efforts and agreements are needed (Resource 20). If we ask our teachers to reflect on their practices, it is only fair that we do the same.

Strengthening Morale

To quote coach Lombardi again, "Build for your team a feeling of oneness, of dependence upon one another, and of strength to be derived from unity" (Lombardi, 2003, p. 184). For a team to be successful, then, the issue is not how well each person works separately but how well people work together. Similarly, a team interacts efficiently and effectively only when the environment lends itself to such. The teacher leader is key in setting the tone and models behaviors congruent to a winning atmosphere.

Yet even if teachers are working and conversing in a professional manner, oftentimes more is necessary. Everyone needs a little cheerleading. What can be frustrating is that *you* are the cheerleader and very rarely will someone cheerlead for you. That is partly what makes this position so draining. But for a team, department, or committee to be successful, there must be a sense of individual and group well-being that should stem from your leadership.

Recognize Individuals.

In my senior English class, about the time when students began receiving college acceptance letters, I would start class by asking if anyone received good news and would be open to sharing it. Students were comfortable with and enjoyed sharing their accomplishments (because community had been established earlier in the year), so much so that I created a poster announcing their successes and future plans. By April, even my underclassmen were interested in checking out the "Big Board" before class and were asking if I would put their names up when they were seniors.

Conduct your meetings the same way. If you are aware of someone presenting a paper at a conference, praise her for it. There will certainly be some who find this practice "cheesy" (and that might be true, but if your team has a strong sense of community, cheesy can even be a good thing), but there will also be those who believe in and appreciate such recognition. And you don't need to confine giving praise to the beginning of a meeting; doing so midway through is a convenient way to break up a meeting (and better ensures that all will be present to share in the celebration) and doing so at the end is a nice way to bring closure.

Increased morale can increase productivity; increased productivity can increase morale.

Some leaders are hesitant to celebrate individual success, achievement, or news publicly because they see it as being unfair to others. This is not necessarily the case. In fact, treating everyone equally can sometimes be the most inequitable thing you can do (think about how you would feel if you were required to turn in lesson plans because someone else had not been engaging in bell-to-bell instruction). It only becomes unfair when you are always recognizing the same person.

However, if you are still reluctant to celebrate individuals, there are ways around this. At one of my inservice sessions, we started with each teacher publicly praising the teacher to the left about something he does well. Even those teachers who didn't get along with each other were able to find some kind of skill or characteristic to commend. We next went around the circle and shared one thing that we were most proud of having accomplished so far during the school year. Responses ranged from reaching certain students to "just surviving." Not only was it important for us to pause and take stock of all that we had achieved, but it served as a valuable team-building and morale-building activity as well.

Offer an Extra Planning Period.

The days after a Back-to-School Night are interminable, especially if you logged a 15-hour day at school by working until conferences began. I can remember one particular conversation that occurred at my car 30 minutes after Back-to-School Night had ended when I foolishly agreed to speak with a parent. Unhappy with my response, she was in the principal's office the very next morning, and the three of us met during my planning period. We all have those days. Imagine how grateful and recharged you would have felt if someone had offered to cover your class later in the day while students were engaged in an activity or taking a test.

Relieve Your Teachers.

If you teach on a block schedule, you are a prisoner of the classroom for about 90 minutes at a stretch. Sometimes it is even impossible to make it to the bathroom in between classes because students need to talk with you. If we're working with young children, our priorities might be more demanding because we may have to clean up after an activity or set up learning stations before the next activity, which sometimes means we may have to wait until lunch to relieve ourselves or get a cup of coffee. All a student has to do to leave for a few minutes is obtain our signature, but we might go through elaborate charades while leaning into the hallway in hopes one of our colleagues will decipher our distress signal, or frantically send an e-mail in case someone is free and sitting at her computer, or decide to simply risk leaving the class alone, an option elementary teachers never have.

Reduce the chance of a negligence lawsuit and demonstrate that you are a compassionate leader by taking a few minutes out of your planning period several times a week to watch someone's class so that he can pull himself together. I once had a teacher who, in order to meet the deadline when senior grades were due, and rather than giving an easy to grade multiple-choice exam, pulled an all-nighter to grade 48 graduating portfolios. The teacher had not told me this, but before first period had even started, I had already heard the story from other teachers (teachers who understood the meaning of community because they were concerned about her well-being). I knew that this teacher would refuse to let me or anyone else relieve her by teaching her classes, so during her second period, I quietly entered the room while she conducted a discussion on theme in *To Kill a Mockingbird* and left a fresh cup of coffee on her desk. I never "insulted" her by offering to cover her classes, but I showed her that I was thinking about her, about the difficult night she had endured and the day she chose not to avoid.

Gift the In-box.

I once taped a scratch-off lottery ticket and a 100 Grand candy bar to a piece of paper and wrote, "I think you're worth at least this much," and then left them (and other "punny" gifts) in each of my teachers' boxes. Some were genuinely touched. Some were more excited by the prospect of winning a couple of bucks. But deep down everyone liked being recognized. I also target individual teachers who I know need a pick-me-up or a grade level team that has worked relentlessly on a project and leave them a Blow Pop with a tag on it that reads, "You rock!"

Meet Out.

Students are stunned when they see us in jeans and outside of a school setting. We joke with them that we sleep in the building and never need to go to the bathroom. Sadly, this is often how we view our colleagues as well, so it can be fun to meet out or set aside a department night where we can see one another as persons with lives outside of school.

At least once a month on a Friday afternoon, my teachers would have a happy hour where we could be ourselves and talk about something other than school. Of course, there were times when the discussion would inevitably drift to an administrator's decision, a troublesome student, or a parent who just didn't understand. You have to know your department; sometimes they need to vent in order to find that common ground, and usually it isn't prudent to do so in the building. Besides, therapeutic as it can be, you don't want the atmosphere in your workroom or lunchroom to become oppressively negative.

An outing at night, however, far from school so that you can change out of work clothes, reduces the chance that you will talk about school. Pick something active such as bowling or pool where people have a chance to talk about what is occurring rather than what has occurred in the building. This allows you to get to know one another as real people, not just as teachers. You might even learn to like one another.

Sponsor a Potluck.

Eating is a social activity. The breaking of bread together is one of our oldest rites of bonding. Whether it is a brown bag, a barbecue, or a formal dinner, we use eating as an excuse to talk to people, so organize a team luncheon. If you have trouble getting people to eat in a central area, hold a potluck on a teacher workday instead of going out for lunch. Save some money, and instead of shouting over the clamor at the local Pizza Hut restaurant, have a professional dialogue in a familial atmosphere. Someone may get to show off a skill no one knew about; someone may proudly present a family recipe for cornbread. Better yet, have a theme lunch or create a good-hearted competition based on trivia questions from your subject area for people to answer while they eat.

Bring Food.

Similar to the above, provide snacks at meetings. If your budget does not allow for it, speak with your administrator. If money is scarce, talk to your PTSA (but inform your principal of your intentions beforehand so that she is not blindsided). Your teachers may even be willing to sponsor food for different meetings. If you are unable to provide food for your meetings, at least have some available at inservice days or other lengthy meetings. Food works wonders, and other groups in the school realize this power by providing food at parent nights, orientations, and the like.

Host a Holiday Party.

Don't underestimate the power of the holidays. Even the biggest Scrooge softens up around this time of year, so you should capitalize on this. Having a department or team party with a Secret Santa adds to the excitement of the holidays and can lift people's spirits. (I realize that schools are not allowed—or it is not acceptable—to use "Christmas break" or "Christmas party," so if you think "Secret Santa" will cause trouble, find a substitute phrase.) Ask your teachers to decide what the maximum cost per gift should be or if the gifts will be gag gifts (because if you don't, there will be at least one disgruntled person who gave a real gift and received a can of shaving cream instead). Put someone in charge of circulating a hat at a meeting or at lunch and draw names. Meet at a local restaurant on the day before break to exchange gifts, or hold a holiday luncheon the day before break (because on the day of break, especially if it is a half day, very few people will want to stick around school). One teacher had such a good time at our holiday party that she still has a picture of herself and her Secret Santa from that evening taped to her filing cabinet.

Cancel a Meeting.

We spend too much time in meetings. The faculty meetings, department meetings, team meetings, grade level meetings, parent conferences, and various committee meetings after the school day has ended, after contract hours, are taxing and draining. The thought of having to listen to more chatter before being able to create a new bulletin board or go home and grade and plan can lead to apathetic behavior at meetings or, worse yet, cause people to fabricate stories about why they cannot attend.

Cancel a meeting once in a while if it is not essential, especially if it is scheduled during a hectic time of the year (midterms need to be graded, for example, or quarter averages are due). Your teachers will appreciate the time you are giving back to them. If the meeting is unavoidable but not necessarily critical, consult your teachers about scheduling it during lunch—if you all share the same lunch—to maximize your time.

Start a Team Newsletter.

A team or department newsletter can be not only a fun way to pass along information but also a vehicle to let your teachers see you as a person. If you don't have the time to write a monthly newsletter, start one up and then rotate the responsibility through the department. Let people write about themselves, their classes, or whatever else they may be interested in. In my newsletters I would often ask a trivia question, and the first person to answer correctly would win a prize. You'd be surprised how excited and involved people became at the prospect of winning a box of overhead transparencies. (See Resource 21.)

Volunteer to Photocopy.

Surprise your teachers when you see them on the way to the copier room by offering to do their photocopying for them. Doing this, or any other small task that takes up their valuable time, can reduce their stress and is another way of showing that you support them. Sometimes just offering is more meaningful than actually doing it. You'll soon find this altruism to be contagious (because you are leading by example), and you will have established a caring and supportive culture.

Reward with Gift Certificates.

Sometimes more than a simple verbal thank-you is necessary for how hard your teachers work. If some have worked intensely to analyze data or pull together a special project and you aren't able to spend your personal funds on rewarding them, investigate the possibility of whether funds exist for you to buy them gift certificates. Even if you can only secure a purchase order for supplies, your teachers will appreciate being appreciated.

Provide Extra Supplies.

Another way to thank teachers is by making sure they always have the supplies available that they need. An abundance of poster board, paper clips, staples, overhead markers, and transparencies is more important than you can imagine. Teachers spend an inordinate amount of money on their classrooms, so if you find a way to prevent them from digging into their own pockets, you will be appreciated as a leader. Many teachers have confessed to me that one of their main frustrations occurs when their chair doesn't stay on top of supply ordering—or, as one teacher expressed, when her chair acts as if it is a major inconvenience to order materials essential to her instruction. Don't ever let this happen in your department because it will have a demoralizing effect.

If teachers are not given the tools they believe are necessary for success, they will feel handcuffed and unsupported. As a result, they might begin perfunctorily performing their job and feel that it is hopeless to achieve success. Just as a team would never be sent onto the playing field without the equipment necessary to win the game, your teachers need to be well equipped. When possible, purchase extra supplies that can be raffled off as a reward at various team-building events.

Design Team Shirts.

Creating a team or department shirt is another way to foster community and boost morale. Display your shirt and team pride on testing days, at pep rallies, or on Fridays (which are usually spirit days in most schools). Or organize a college sweatshirt Friday where your teachers wear a sweatshirt from their alma mater. This can promote unity in addition to sending a great message to students.

Make It up to Your Teachers.

If one of your teachers had a difficult year because of a heavy schedule, a particular class, a teaming situation, or something else, try to make it up to her for the following year. Meet her scheduling needs first or make sure you hear her scheduling concerns. Do your best to ensure positive morale by recognizing when your teachers were martyrs and giving them a better year.

Throw a Year-End Party.

Teachers flee the building at the end of the year, almost as if there were a contest of who can leave first. Establish a year-end party so that people will look forward to something rather than look forward to leaving. Celebrate your individual and team efforts and successes—in some cases, success might mean having just survived the year.

References

Lombardi, V., Jr. (2003). *What it takes to be #1: Vince Lombardi on leadership.* New York: McGraw-Hill.

6

Instructional Leadership

Improving Student and Teacher Achievement

Just before I started as department chair, I had heard through the grapevine that the standardized test scores would never improve because the students weren't capable of higher achievement. Hearing this a few days before I began rattled me. Had I made the correct decision in leaving a comfortable position in another district? Had I bitten off more than I could chew? What if this person was right? Would I be ending my career in a new county before it had even started?

I discovered, however, that although a large portion of the student population had language deficiencies and we were facing many external obstacles (lack of parental involvement, a high rate of students who received free and reduced lunches, gang activity, and so on), our low scores did not necessarily reflect what our students knew or could do. The belief that the students could not handle the work became a self-fulfilling prophecy that teachers were all too willing to buy into. It was easier for them to believe that it was the students' fault or the sum of all the negatives they faced than to rework lesson plans, rethink their philosophies, or grow as professionals. Our low scores also reflected problems in the instructional program.

What I learned, and perhaps always knew, is that student achievement begins and ends with the quality of the teacher, the instructional program, and its leadership. So in trying to improve achievement, you first need to consider whether your teachers are effective. Are they instructionally solid? How do you determine whether they are or are not? What do you do if they are not? Are your teachers open to new ideas? What do your teachers do if their students are underperforming?

Whether you are a team leader in an elementary or middle school or a department chair in a high school, one of your primary roles as a teacher leader is instructional leadership, so at some point you will need to reflect on and answer these questions. But while you evaluate your teachers, your teachers will be evaluating you: they will be deciding whether they respect your instructional leadership. If your teachers do not respect you instructionally, you will find it difficult to succeed as a leader.

Although your lessons or activities do not always need to be perfect, your lessons should exhibit best practices. You model bell-to-bell instruction, you differentiate instruction, and you provide remediation. Furthermore, your fellow teachers must see you as a specialist in your content area. If you are a history teacher, you can speak knowledgeably about the Magna Carta, the War of 1812, and the New Deal; if you are an English teacher, medieval literature, Puritanism, gothic romance, and so on. Your teachers need to be able to trust your judgment when you make suggestions regarding the department's curriculum or an individual teacher's objectives, lesson plans, and assessments.

Your fellow teachers need to view you as a resource, someone they seek out for equipment, literature, and ancillary materials. You represent a treasure chest of ideas and are eager to share them. At best, you have taught all grade and ability levels, so you are able to relate to every teacher in your department. If you are needed to cover a class, any class in your department or on your grade level, you would be able to step in and teach, not just follow an emergency lesson plan. The students would not suffer for not having their classroom teacher that day.

If you haven't taught all the electives that your department offers, you have studied their aspects, understand their objectives, and comprehend their nuances. As an instructional leader, you not only are knowledgeable of innovative instructional techniques but also understand how students learn and have demonstrated success in your own classroom. You are a true coach in that you understand all facets of the game and how to bring out the skills of all your players. It is an overwhelming charge.

The Effective Classroom

Discussing what constitutes an effective classroom is certainly a broad topic. I don't attempt to cover every aspect of the subject; rather I stress its characteristics and importance. As an instructional leader, your focus should be on ensuring solid instruction and serving your students with a curriculum that meets their needs: the two most direct ways to influence student achievement.

Observe and Coach Your Teachers.

Administrators are so bogged down by their numerous responsibilities that they often don't have the chance to visit classrooms as much as they would like. Few educators enter administration because they are eager to deal with discipline and irate parents; administration is appealing to them because they enjoy seeing good teaching and helping teachers grow. But this is not always possible.

Your role as instructional leader can be to act as a surrogate for your administrator. If you were to volunteer to visit classrooms— not to evaluate but to observe—and give your administrator feedback on what is occurring on your team or in your department, he would surely appreciate your assistance. Moreover, you have a vested interest in seeing your teachers succeed because you are the person most responsible for your department's instructional program—so anything you can do to enhance their chances for success is to your advantage.

However, your teachers might not be as open to this idea as you are. First and foremost, you need to stress to your teachers that your observing their classes is not to catch them doing something wrong but instead doing something right. Your role is to reinforce the positive things you see and provide feedback when it is asked for. If you still face some concerns, then avoid drop-ins and have your teachers pick a particular class for you to observe. Meet with these teachers ahead of time so they can walk you through the lesson if that will put them more at ease.

Now, even if you take these steps, you still might observe things that need to be corrected; that is not your main function for entering the classroom, though. If you witness questionable practices, then the prudent thing to do is to turn this information over to your administrator. In many ways, observing your teachers is similar to hosting a practicum student: when you work with a practicum student, you try to find ways to support her and help her grow. If severe problems arise, you function as a conduit to the supervising professor who will, based on your input, address these issues.

Present yourself as a partner, someone who has an equal stake in things going well.

But it needn't always get that far. When you meet with your teachers after the observation, make it clear that you would rather handle issues between the two of you before they have a chance to escalate to the main office. As I tell my teachers, I have an interest in seeing them do well and in rectifying problems. If I don't, our supervisor will become involved, and I'm sure everyone would rather not have that happen. When phrased this way, most teachers who are nervous about having you come into their classrooms, or those who are concerned that you are overstepping your boundaries, might be grateful that you are trying to take care of problems in-house.

After your observation, you should address what went well during the class. Let that be the question you lead with: "What do you think went well with the lesson I observed?" As an instructional leader and effective classroom teacher, you are already familiar with the ingredients for a successful class. Yet sometimes we are so closely involved with our own classes that we take these elements for granted.

First of all, your more effective teachers have a set routine in their classes. Students are aware of and familiar with the established routine. They know how and where to find assignments and make-up work, they are ready for a warm-up at the beginning of the class that will reinforce the previous lesson or introduce a new one, and the environment is one that supports and promotes learning either through the display of student work or examples of model work. The atmosphere is one of inquiry, and classroom management minimizes disruptions rather than escalating them.

The teacher does not barricade himself behind the lectern or desk for 90 minutes but breaks up the period by guiding at least two different activities related to a common objective. Students are engaged and are given the opportunity to create meaning rather than have it forced upon them. Both student and teacher investigate answers instead of relying on rote answers. An observable rapport exists between student and teacher that sparks inquiry, that makes the class a learning community, that assists in classroom management. And lessons include some kind of closure in the form of reviewing material, filling out exit slips, or beginning homework.

Perhaps all these features are not observable in every class period, but you should be able to see traces of them. More than likely your teacher will be able to identify them as well, so when you meet with her after the observation, simply reinforce the lesson's strengths by providing specific comments and let her do most of the talking. When addressing areas of growth, ask her, "Is there anything that you wish would have gone a little better?" Most teachers, like students when they complete self-assessments, are harder on themselves than we would be. In fact, you'll discover that many teachers would rather begin the post-observation meeting by immediately commenting on what they believe went wrong. Either they are so cognizant of what went poorly or are so concerned with clearing things up that they jump to this first.

Your purpose in observing the class is not to point out what the teacher did poorly, but don't ignore the opportunity to help him grow. Discuss what he perceives the lesson's shortcomings to be.

Offer assistance and resources, but try to have him take ownership of any missteps by identifying the causes and brainstorming solutions. If he claims there were no missteps, then don't push it. You're not likely to convince him then and there of what you think, so if you try, you run the risk of escalating the situation. To document your observation, although it won't be official and can't be placed in his file, you might want to follow up with a memo (Resource 22).

Map the Curriculum.

How familiar is the following scenario: you were hired right out of college, obtained a job a few weeks before the school year started, and were told that you would be teaching 9th and 11th grade. You were given copies of the state and local objectives, teacher editions, and maybe even paired with a mentor. But when all was said and done, you needed to develop lesson plans, activities, and assessments for a curriculum that was largely unfamiliar to you. Sure, you were comfortable with the content, but in terms of what exactly needed to be taught, or how it could be successfully taught, that was a little cloudy. As a good teacher is apt to do, you found your footing—maybe not immediately, but you eventually discovered how long a unit would take and strategies for teaching it.

Imagine if instead you had been handed a curriculum map when you began your first job. This guide would have outlined the essential knowledge for a particular grade level, suggested various activities and learning extensions, and offered a plan on how to organize your year. You would have been better set up for success, and, as a result, so would have your students.

Some educators bristle at the notion of a curriculum map because they fear that they will lose their autonomy and creativity. This is not the case. The basic definition of a map is that it shows the various routes to a destination: how you choose to get there is up to you. Therefore, you need to demonstrate to your teachers that having such a guide still allows them freedom. An introductory page to the map or an explanatory section might be helpful and allay their concerns.

A curriculum map should be a resource for your teachers—a manageable resource at that, not something cumbersome and difficult to access and digest, which will cause it to lie untouched in filing cabinets. Nor should it be a way to micromanage what occurs in classrooms; instead, it should give a teacher an idea of how long a certain unit will take to cover and help him pace out his year. A curriculum map does not state what should be occurring every week but rather charts curriculum over the course of a quarter or a semester, leaving the teacher the flexibility to explore other areas and to extend learning. One of the advantages of a curriculum map is that it tightens the curriculum and better aligns your program horizontally and vertically, a benefit to both students and teachers. It does not mandate what material should be taught, but offers suggestions based on what has sparked student interest in the past, what teachers have found to be effective, and what best matches with prescribed objectives.

To ensure that the map is not perceived as a top-down directive, invite your teachers to participate in creating it. Ask them to bring successful lessons, assessments, and other resources to a team or department meeting and consider the following:

- What are the big-ticket items for this unit? Meaning, what should every student know or be able to do at the end of the unit/marking period/semester?
- What are the essential questions that will guide our focus and enhance student interest and inquiry?
- Are there other topics we might want to cover along the way to our destination? Are there areas that will complement the key ideas and issues of a unit?
- What are the pertinent objectives?
- How will we know we achieved our objectives? How will we measure student success or assess learning?
- What materials could we use to get students to that point?
- How much time do we estimate needing to cover this area of study?

- How will we organize the curriculum? Thematically, chronologically, or some other way?

Your curriculum map shouldn't be so specific that teachers feel they have no choice or control over what they do in their classrooms, but it should be explicit in that it illustrates the team's expectations. This is important because when one class or grade level deviates, it creates a ripple effect throughout the instructional program that could take years to undo.

Make curriculum mapping an ongoing process by revisiting, reevaluating, and revising maps regularly throughout the school year, while successes and failures are still fresh in the mind, rather than at isolated moments. Analyzing data from the end of a unit or a semester test or

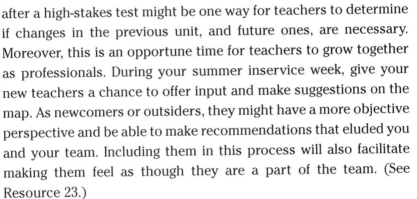

A curriculum map should be a living document.

after a high-stakes test might be one way for teachers to determine if changes in the previous unit, and future ones, are necessary. Moreover, this is an opportune time for teachers to grow together as professionals. During your summer inservice week, give your new teachers a chance to offer input and make suggestions on the map. As newcomers or outsiders, they might have a more objective perspective and be able to make recommendations that eluded you and your team. Including them in this process will also facilitate making them feel as though they are a part of the team. (See Resource 23.)

Remediation

Even in the most effective classroom, there are those students who do not achieve. With the advent of No Child Left Behind, gone are the days of saying, "Well, I taught the material—he just didn't get it." Gone are the days of proclaiming that students have a right to fail. Gone are the days of hiding behind the statement that a student did not bother to come after school for help. Gone are the days of saying it is not our fault (whether or not it is true). This new era of accountability is forcing teachers to examine their classroom practices, to scrutinize their students' and their own behavior.

Some teachers are uncomfortable with this. Others welcome the opportunity for someone to analyze what goes on in their classrooms. It frustrates both groups that, because of high-stakes testing, there seems to be precious little time to go back and reteach material to ensure that every student has mastered the essential skills. Even if students are new to our country, are working several grade levels below average, have horrific home situations, or simply do not care, the current reality is that we are expected to find ways to remediate them.

A good instructional leader helps his teachers understand the need to analyze and reflect on their practices, and offers support and resources when his teachers face obstacles to student success. He is also proactive. He talks informally throughout the quarter with his teachers to see how their students are doing, what problems they are facing, and what help or support they need. But the effective instructional leader does more than that. Although it can be extremely time-consuming, he meets with his teachers to determine why students are not succeeding and brainstorms solutions and strategies with them.

Discussions with my teachers produced the following general reasons for why students do not achieve: lack of regular school attendance, lack of completed homework or class work, lack of parental involvement, lack of student motivation, and lack of skills. There are probably other reasons, but we were able to develop a checklist of strategies to address these areas and help remediate students (Resource 24). When we were asked by administrators what we had done for our failing students, we could point to the multitude of strategies we had used. Although each school has unique obstacles, below are general strategies that can be adapted.

Acknowledge Ability Levels.

A few years ago, a colleague expressed frustration that her department chair required all freshmen to read *A Tale of Two Cities*. She wanted her students to be exposed to the classics, but she had discovered through a reading pre-test she had administered during the initial weeks of school that nearly all the students were reading sharply below grade level. She had chosen to teach in this underperforming, inner-city school because she wanted to help students the system had forgotten. Her charge was challenging enough due to apathy, an absent school infrastructure, scant supplies, and many other marks of impoverished, failing schools, but then she also had to contend with a department chair who was obsessed with creating a rigorous curriculum at the expense of the students. Hard as she tried, regardless of how talented an educator she was, her students could not comprehend the prescribed text and failed miserably.

Instead of building up her students' skills, which is what her instincts told her to do, she was forced to plow ahead with the curriculum her chair had imposed on the department. Exasperated, she left at the end of the year; unfortunately, her students were left behind as well. Wanting all students to read Charles Dickens is admirable, but this leader ignored the needs of the students in his department. Work should pose an intellectual challenge, not an intellectual obstacle. If he had focused on giving the students a solid foundation and scaffolding the curriculum, they would have had a better chance at success. Give your students what they need. If they are starving, you must first feed them before you can teach them how to cook for themselves.

Differentiate Instruction.

Even before high-stakes testing began to move into the educational spotlight, differentiation was gaining attention because many schools were dissolving homogenous classes in favor of heterogeneous grouping, and teachers were struggling to reach all these learners in one class. Many teachers interpret differentiation to mean using a variety of instructional strategies and assessments, but it encompasses more than that. It is flexibly grouping students— both homogenously and heterogeneously—when necessary and designing lessons appropriate for each group. This can be a challenging task because you are in essence creating several different lesson plans under the umbrella of one lesson. However, the past practice of just shuffling along the 5 students in a class of 28 who did not achieve mastery during a unit does not serve all students.

As an instructional leader, you should be able to provide presentations, literature, materials, or some kind of resource system for your teachers. Although most teachers are familiar with teaching to the different multiple intelligences, some might feel uncomfortable with this type of planning and delivery and will need your assistance and support for when they decide to step outside of their comfort zone. Tap someone who has successfully taught a lesson that incorporated flexible ability grouping to present it to your team. Encourage team members to welcome colleagues into their classrooms and encourage teachers to observe their colleagues: peer observation can be a powerful form of staff development and a way to help us better reach students.

Reteach and Retest.

When students do not fare well, frequently a teacher's response is one of two scenarios. She announces to the class that she will offer a retake and gives the same test. Students try to memorize the correct answers to the questions they missed and then regurgitate the material a couple of days later. Or she announces that she will give another test, and she does. But that is all she does. She does nothing to address the areas where students did not succeed, so how could they pass the test the second time around?

You need to help your teachers see that when a large percentage of students are not demonstrating mastery during a unit of study, then the material needs to be retaught. That does not mean simply *covering* the material again. Instead, it involves finding other ways for students to access the material, analyzing practices, reconfiguring lesson plans, trying new ideas, and seeking help or suggestions from colleagues who had success during the same unit.

Use Assessments as Teaching Tools.

Too often teachers merely return graded work, doing nothing else with it. Even if a teacher's students achieved a proficient level of competency, he still should use returned work as an opportunity for students to learn and as a tool for further assessment. Students can be paired together and talk about how they arrived at an answer; students can write out responses to incorrect, and even correct, answers; and students can participate in a general class discussion about the assessment. The point is that assessments should not be isolated events. They need to be discussed, used as teaching tools, and referenced in the future.

Establish Tutoring Programs.

Sometimes it is just not possible to remediate all students within the classroom. Students might have such low skills that they need more individualized attention or extended practice to build these skills. Although tutoring was available in my building through the National Honor Society and other such groups, my department created a more structured after-school program so that we could target certain areas of need. We created a 12-week program that focused on different objectives, strands, and skills each week (Resource 25). We were unable to be paid for our time, but nearly all saw the benefits of such a program and agreed to donate 90 minutes once during the year to teach a session.

The teacher responsible for any given week's tutoring session needed very little preparation because a leadership position that came to be known as the SOL review coordinator evolved out of our efforts. The coordinator asked colleagues to bring successful lessons and ideas to a department meeting and then organized the material into a resource book. Between that and various skill-building workbooks, we had ample resources each week to help reach our students. The lessons and materials were housed in a giant loose-leaf binder, and with only minor modifications, we were able to duplicate the program each year.

Even though we had the materials and teacher support necessary for such a program, we still needed to create ways to entice students to attend. We presented our idea to the PTSA and were able to secure money for this cause, which was critical. Snacks and soda attracted the students, and, using donations from local businesses and gift certificates, we would raffle off prizes at the end of the session or create friendly competitions. We publicized the program by mailing home a letter and posting flyers around the building, and teachers offered their students extra credit for attending. Each teacher and tutor personally invited students, and parents were also called to help ensure that we were attracting the students who would most benefit from the program.

This program did not replace one-on-one tutoring before and after school because that too was a valuable method for remediating students. Although such a program is not a cure-all for problems that students and teachers face, it is another important support system to help students succeed in class and on high-stakes tests.

Consider Creative Scheduling.

Tutoring does not always need to take place after school. In the early fall of 2002, the school plan committee suggested we implement a mentoring program in our building. When the Instructional Council began discussing this idea, it became obvious that we would need to restructure the school day to accommodate such a program. As we discussed different scheduling options and examined what neighboring schools did, we discovered that changing the schedule could maximize student learning because it could allow us additional time to remediate or work with students.

By the end of the year, we had settled on a schedule that reduced passing time and shaved a few minutes off each period to give us a 35-minute, rotating period that we called PAWS, Performance Activities with Students—a play on the word "pause," because the school day would in essence pause midway through, as well as on our mascot, the jaguar. Over the course of seven days, a student would report once to each of his classes to make up quizzes, seek extra help, or even tutor other students. This helped us reduce the number of students who were failing for not completing make-up work, and it alleviated the amount of time a teacher would spend working with students after school (additionally, it benefited those students who were unable to stay after school because of transportation issues or because they had jobs or other obligations).

Teach Study Skills.

We often take for granted that our students know and understand concepts and skills that we view as elementary, so it might surprise you how many students do not know how to survey and skim a chapter, how to use subject headings, or even what a dictionary can tell them about a word other than the definition. Perhaps no one taught us how to take notes when we were students, but we found a way to create a system for note taking that helped us succeed. Maybe that is why we assume that our students have effective note-taking skills or will be able to figure them out on their own.

Unfortunately, most do not, so it is a good idea to teach and review outlining, clustering, brainstorming, or another system of note taking that will help students access and digest material in order to become better learners. Moreover, few students have been taught listening skills—cues such as emphasis and repetition and key words—so they are lost not only when a teacher presents material but also when they work in cooperative groups or when peers present material. Teaching students how to organize a notebook and use a planner helps them learn organizational and time management skills, a basic component of remediation. Only when a student is equipped with the skills essential to success can she feel comfortable and confident that she will achieve success.

Make Work Meaningful.

Students need to see a connection between the subject material and their lives. You can effectively forge this link through essential questions. At the beginning of a unit, pose a thought-provoking question or questions that will inspire student interest. To say that we will study U.S. history because it meets a state objective is not likely to create much interest for students, nor for teachers. But teachers who begin the year by asking questions that will guide instruction and inquiry—"What does it mean to be an American?"

"What is the American dream and how do you relate to it?" "How has the United States changed throughout the past two hundred years?"—have a better chance of increasing student interest and tapping into a variety of student backgrounds.

Teachers who are able to show students the real-world significance or applicability of what they are learning are able to increase student motivation. For example, science teachers in my building held a science fair where student-guided experiments were displayed for parents and the community; math students created portfolios where they demonstrated how geometrical rules affected their lives; English teachers and their students wrote letters to the school paper and posted online reviews of books. On the whole, students were more active and enthused by these projects; they better related to them because they saw how the work was applicable beyond the school walls. Even with high-stakes testing hanging over students' heads, it is no longer possible to say that they will study something simply because they have to or are told to; encourage your teachers to engage students in meaningful ways that also satisfy local and state requirements.

Begin Homework in Class.

When discussing student achievement with my teachers, I discovered that one of the main reasons students were failing was that they were not completing any homework. In talking with many students, I found that it wasn't about understanding homework or being able to find the time to complete it. As one student confided, homework "just wasn't fun."

I am confident that this is the case in schools across the nation. Some districts have now chosen homework as their next target for elimination on the educational landscape because they believe that homework—not student or parent attitudes toward it (or even toward education in general)—is an obstacle to success. These knee-jerk pedagogical reactions in an attempt to improve student performance actually do a disservice to students. Homework is an essential part of learning, so engaging in meaningful—the key word being meaningful—homework should enhance a student's chances at success.

But when even meaningful homework becomes an impediment, you need to reach a compromise rather than totally leveling the practice. First, develop a departmental or team statement regarding homework that both students and parents are aware of. For example, teachers can include it on their syllabi. At Falls Church High School, we also posted the following on our Web site:

> Homework is an integral part of the learning process, and as such, the English department believes in assigning regular, meaningful homework to reinforce skills and material from class as well as to prepare for future classes. Homework generally takes the form of the following:
> - Active reading
> - Practice with vocabulary and literary skills
> - Long-term essays and projects
>
> Students and parents should be familiar with the policies of the county and their teachers concerning late work.

By outlining to parents what homework consists of, you will be alleviating their concerns and informing them of what they should expect their children to do at home. (And think about how often you've heard parents say, "Johnny always says that he doesn't have any homework—what can or should he be doing at home?")

Making your expectations clear from the beginning of school, announcing deadlines well in advance in a variety of ways, and teaching students how to pace themselves and how to organize their time is an essential strategy for improving achievement. To help students manage their homework and workload, consider creating a Web site where they can download assignments. Or investigate the possibility of your school purchasing software such as Blackboard (a forum where students can keep up with work, submit assignments, participate in online discussions, and use calendar and task tools to get organized), and lead a session for your team or tap one of your teachers to lead a session on its use.

Opponents of homework are eager to dismiss the practice in schools that have a high rate of students who receive free and reduced lunches, which many interpret to mean an inability or an indifference of a parent to assist with homework. Parents being unable to assist with homework should not pose a problem because the homework should not be new material, but rather something that has already been covered in class. True, it would be ideal if all parents could structure a conducive learning environment for their children at home, but this doesn't always occur even in affluent areas.

To purge the practice of homework denies students the opportunity to improve their study skills, to be more disciplined learners, and to work with important material (not to mention it is a method of teaching responsibility to a generation that is constantly being absolved of it). If educators are truly intent on increasing enrollment in advanced classes and by extension matriculating more students into college, then we are harming these students by removing homework from our programs, because homework and independent study are core elements of higher education. You might not be able to dissuade these challengers, so giving students time in class to begin their work can show that your department understands external obstacles while maintaining its integrity and commitment to excellence. And allowing students 10 minutes at the end of class to begin their homework is an effective way of monitoring student progress and providing closure to a lesson.

Create Incentives.

Teachers often do things in their classes that they and their students take for granted. Maybe we allow students to have food in class, we do without a seating chart, or something else along those lines. Rather than freely handing out such privileges in class, use them as incentives with your students. We already do this for classroom management purposes, so it seems natural to do so for academic reasons. Granted, we want students to see the value of learning and education, and some literature cautions against using external motivation with students. But if we refuse to recognize that this generation of students is primarily motivated by external factors rather than internal ones, we will continue to ignore a means of helping students achieve. Those who argue that this reduces learning to simple reward and punishment conveniently ignore that many students are already motivated by grades, whether it is striving toward an *A* or just doing enough to earn a *D*.

Using incentives and privileges as a form of motivation can help a student experience success; once she experiences success, she becomes more receptive to learning. One of my colleagues teaches a class of students with low interest, low reading abilities that failed at least two of their previous year's SOL tests. She promised them a pizza party if everyone passed the next test. To her amazement, the lowest score was an 85. These students bragged to their friends and other teachers that they were going to have a pizza party because they had done so well. Even though she didn't make such a promise for the next test, and some students did not fare as well, all students learned a valuable lesson: that they were capable of success.

Not all incentives have to feel similar to bribery, however. Create a review game based on the game show "Jeopardy," and, if you want, assign homework passes or points to the winning team that translate into extra credit. Using a talk show format or adapting games such as Pictionary, Taboo, and Bingo can be a fun way to review material prior to a test. Learning is a right, but having fun while learning is not, so this can be a powerful way to motivate students.

Cultivate Community in the Classroom.

Sometimes students underperform because they lack motivation. Even when the material is relevant to their lives and lessons are engaging and interesting, they still feel disconnected from a class. One way to combat feelings of apathy is to create trust- and team-building activities for the first few days of school. Another way is to give students a greater voice in your class. This can be done on the very first day of school by inviting students to help construct classroom rules. In addition, setting aside a period once a quarter for a class meeting—a time to encourage general (yet orderly) discussions, to address concerns, or just to let students express themselves—helps create a caring, supportive environment where students can feel a sense of belonging. This can be a powerful tool for enhancing motivation and, by extension, achievement.

Administer a survey to your classes, similar to ones we completed in college at the end of a course, where students can respond anonymously to the pacing, style of instruction, and general atmosphere of the class (Resource 26). After pulling together the data, hold a class meeting to share the results and use them as a springboard for students to talk honestly about their perceptions and feelings—and for you to talk about yours. One colleague shares the results of her surveys and suggestions with the next year's class. Receiving a handout entitled "Tips from the Trenches," her students feel as if they have been given a kind of cheat sheet, which increases their motivation and their belief that they can succeed.

A feeling of community and motivation can also be created when you display student work, celebrate student achievement, and demonstrate personal interest in students' lives. Invite administrators to watch student presentations or show them student work. Projects displayed in the classroom and hallway are evidence of positive activity and growth (as well as good PR, given the various people and groups who use the building). Take an interest in your students' lives and accomplishments outside the classroom. As a colleague once told me, students don't care what we know until they know that we care. Attend games and other extracurricular events or greet students and say good-bye to them at the door on a daily basis. Such actions are powerful means of demonstrating your interest and increasing student motivation. Many students ultimately want to please their teachers, and once they see that we care more about them than about grades and test scores, they will respect us more and be more willing to achieve.

Inform Students of Their Progress.

Too often, students only know what their grades are when interim grades, progress reports, or report cards are mailed home.

Students should receive grade sheets once a week or every other week so that they are aware of their progress. Although it might sound obvious, students need to have their grades explained to them. For example, we may understand that a student's grades of a "100" and a "0" for the marking period will give him an average of a "50," but a student might not realize this or understand why his average is so low after "just one missing assignment."

Create a self-guiding activity for your class to allow yourself time to meet with your students individually. Explain the grade they earned and help them identify causes of failure, areas for improvement, and what motivates them. Use codenames or pin numbers to protect your students' privacy and post their averages in your classroom on a weekly basis. Require students who are underperforming to have a grade sheet or assignment signed by a parental figure. Be sure to follow up with someone at home if a signature is not returned so that students know you are not making empty threats.

Communicate Frequently with Parents.

Keeping only students informed of their grades is like bringing only half of the team to the game: the coaches need to be involved as well, because no matter how good the players are, their coaches are an essential part of success. Keeping track of which parents we need to call (and which phone numbers are working), playing phone tag, and documenting calls can drain us more than our classroom obligations do. But as frustrating as this part of our job can be, parental communication is integral in helping a student succeed. Because parents are capable of turning a student around by exerting pressure (usually in the form of incentives or reward and punishment), they sometimes need to be invited to the game and cajoled through our persistence and insistence into joining.

At my school, we were fortunate that when a parent did not speak English, we could use translators in our school system to facilitate communication. If such a resource is not available, find students who can make an initial phone call informing parents that they will need to bring a translator to a conference because there is an academic problem. Your team might also look into the possibility of creating a form letter that can be translated into several different languages. And encourage teachers to help one another with phone calls, even if it is only to make parents aware that they need to contact their child's classroom teacher.

Involve the Guidance Department.

Inviting guidance counselors into the fold gives you access to other resources. Not only might a guidance counselor be knowledgeable of extenuating circumstances, but she also might be able to refer students to someone else who can help. Sometimes counselors are capable of talking with parents in ways that we as teachers are unable to because they have a different kind of rapport with the family or simply because they are removed from the situation. A good counselor knows her students well. If you can bring another adult into the picture who cares about a student's success, who can help monitor his progress, and who can exert pressure when he needs it, then you have enlisted the help of a significant support system.

Assess Your Assessments.

What are your teachers testing? Even if your teachers are instructionally sound, are they testing essential knowledge? What do their assessments consist of? For example, English is a unique discipline because the content, in many ways, is irrelevant: there are no state objectives in Virginia that mandate that every student read *Lord of the Flies*. Teachers on every grade level have a certain amount of flexibility in choosing what material they teach, but at the end of a quarter, semester, or year, every student should possess the same set of skills. After my department adopted the idea of having midterms, some exams tested students on isolated, obscure information. Is it necessary for a student to be able to identify four months later a minor piece of information from Chapter 4 of *Lord of the Flies*? Certainly not. Should a student be able to explain William Golding's modes of characterization or how he develops a symbol over the course of the novel? Most definitely.

Sometimes even good teachers don't know what to test, so your job is to ensure that students are being tested on what is important. Assessments should be aligned with state and local standards and should reflect unit objectives. This is true for all disciplines. In social studies, where content is crucial, a teacher's exams might reveal what is really being taught in the class and provide you with an idea if something in the curriculum needs to be corrected or if the teacher needs to be steered away from hobby teaching. One colleague, frustrated by others who gave easier exams and did not always assess students on essential knowledge, initiated the idea of a "challenge check." Each teacher brought a copy of a unit test to a team meeting so that teachers could collaborate and share test questions. It gave people a better idea of what was going on in each classroom and whether others were injecting the same level of rigor into their assessments.

Assessments should be used to gauge progress, not to punish students or teachers.

Such an idea has the potential of rubbing some teachers the wrong way, but those who are defensive about this are generally the ones who need the most help in tweaking their assessments. You certainly don't want your teachers to walk away from a meeting feeling bruised, but in this high-stakes era you don't want to ignore problems in favor of preserving feelings and egos. If you still face resistance after trying to help your teachers understand the necessity of accurate assessments, then there is very little else that can be done other than presenting the problem to your supervisor.

A doctor administers blood work in order to diagnose how well her patient is or to determine the cause of an illness, not to blame him for getting sick. She discusses strengths and weaknesses in his lifestyle to help him understand how to be healthier, not to punish him. She does not rely on a single blood test to assess his health; she will run other tests or have him perform activities to determine how physically fit he is. A doctor will never assess her patient on his effort, abilities, or potential, let alone on his behavior in the office. Patients in specific age groups should be able to perform certain functions and fall within acceptable ranges, but a good doctor will consider the patient's history and other factors instead of solely comparing him to other patients or a statistic.

The same applies to your teachers. Their assessments should diagnose students' strengths and weaknesses and consequently inform goal setting and future unit and lesson planning. Students should not be graded on their behavior in the classroom, on how "healthy" they could be, or on whether they tried their hardest on a test. It can be unnerving to eliminate these things from the grade book, because it will typically lower a teacher's average GPA. So if a teacher is accurately assessing student performance, don't let anyone judge his effectiveness simply based on his quarter grades, just as one would not evaluate a doctor based on whether his patients were overweight.

Even though promotion is most often linked to standardized test scores, your teachers should use other forms of assessment. In disciplines where facts and information are highly valued, students should also have to apply their knowledge to new scenarios and tasks. They should be made aware of the goals and criteria ahead of time (it should never be taken for granted that they know what a teacher is looking for). Furthermore, a strong instructional leader will help his teachers implement rubrics in their classrooms, rubrics that students have a voice in creating or rubrics that are uniform and consistent across the grade level.

Although students will eventually have to pass a pencil and paper test, alternative forms of assessment can be instrumental in helping them to pass such tests. Of course, one of the main drawbacks with a high-stakes test is that it is a one-shot evaluation of what a student knows, understands, or can do. We have no control over that, but we do have some control over what occurs in our departments or on our teams.

Ensure that your teachers not only assess students in a variety of ways but also assess them frequently. Using unit tests as the sole assessments does a disservice to the student and yields little information about classroom practices. Exit cards, quizzes, conferences, projects, portfolios, and anecdotal notes can be more useful forms of assessment because they can indicate what a student needs in order to be successful and can enhance the potential for success, whereas a unit test will only corroborate our impressions. Ongoing assessment will give your teachers a better picture of what is going on in their classrooms and will allow them to focus on growth rather than on isolated achievement.

Along these lines, have your teachers pre-assess students at the beginning of the year to determine their strengths and weaknesses. Then at the end of quarters and at midterms they will have baseline data to gauge their students' growth. In addition, your teachers will have a better idea of what their students need and will be able to tailor the pace and focus of future lessons.

Alternative and ongoing assessments should not be seen as "dumbing down" the curriculum, so make it clear to your teachers that they should continue to have high expectations, but they should temper them with leniency and generosity. Just as teachers are not dismissed because of one quarter's worth of poor grades, their students should not be evaluated solely on one test.

Implement Sustained Silent Reading.

Too many educators see reading as strictly an area that affects English or language arts. Teachers and administrators are quick to relegate the problem of literacy to English teachers, but if a student is not achieving in his English class, then the odds are that he is not achieving in his biology or history class due to his low reading abilities. In a culture becoming more and more dominated by non-readers, you must help your students succeed by leading the war against illiteracy. Although a math teacher might not necessarily know how to remediate a student so that he can better understand word problems, she can take a step in helping her students by implementing a Sustained Silent Reading (SSR) program in her department.

Promote independent reading and model it in your department's classrooms. There will inevitably be some teachers who are opposed to setting aside valuable instructional time for students to read in class, but the reality is that because students are seduced by new and improved distractions such as video games and the Internet, reading at home occurs less and less (and in many cases, not at all). Because this is the case, it makes sense to give students time during the school day for them to practice reading and build their skills. If a teacher can turn a student on to a book, then perhaps that student will develop or nurture a love for reading, which will ultimately help him over his entire academic career.

One of teachers' main concerns is how to monitor SSR. Experts say that assignments or assessments should not be punitive, meaning that students should not be graded down for not completing their SSR. At the very least, though, you need to establish a system to track what students are doing (Resource 27).

Be Aware of Cheating.

There has been a flurry of articles in recent years about students and cheating. It is easy to think that increased cheating is mainly a result of increased technology, that the more high-tech we become, the easier it is for students to find shortcuts to completing projects and papers. Regardless of whether this is true, students still cheat on tests, class work, and homework, and their attitudes toward cheating need to be addressed. In this day and age of instant gratification, students rarely have to work hard for what they want, so when it comes to completing work for class, they try to find the shortcut—oftentimes not because they do not understand the work nor because their home life is an obstacle to success, but because they have been conditioned to find the easy way out, especially if something does not strike them as "fun."

Think about how many times you have heard students talking about assignments in the hallways: "Sure, you can copy my homework," "Did Johnny do the homework? I really need to get it from him," and the like. Recent phenomenon or not, the reality is that students do not consider sharing or copying homework as cheating: it is simply an easier way to achieve a goal. This is not a problem endemic to honors or advanced classes; it is a problem in all classes. In fact, a colleague explained to me that in his daughter's

1st grade class in a nearby district, students take all tests at study carols because teachers discovered that students were copying answers from their neighbors' answer sheets. First graders!

At least those administrators and teachers recognized that there was a problem. Leaders who don't want to admit that this epidemic exists do not understand why some of their students do not succeed in class or on high-stakes tests. For example, if a student has copied homework all marking period but then fails the unit tests, he is still more than likely to pass for the quarter. But he is also more than likely to fail a barrier test. Talk with your teachers, administrators, and parents about this problem and make your department's stance clear.

Not all students cheat for the same reason: some cheat because of the high competition to get into a good school, whereas others cheat because they do not understand the work that is asked of them. If we turn a blind eye to this practice because we cannot be bothered or we refuse to believe it exists, then our students will be in even greater need for remediation.

High-Stakes Testing

Whether the No Child Left Behind Act remains intact or evolves into something else, accountability and standardized testing will continue to be a driving force in education for years to come. Although I am confident that educators have read and heard enough about standardized testing, related issues—which are sometimes overlooked, ignored, or forgotten—must be addressed because they can affect test results.

Take Tests Seriously.

Although the prospect of earning a diploma should be motivation enough to take a high-stakes test seriously, some students are so myopic that they are unable to see far enough ahead to graduation. All they understand is the here and now. Other students might not plan to finish high school but are still required to take the high-stakes test, and their scores still count toward a school's accreditation. They may be capable of passing the test, but that is no guarantee that they will take it seriously. And even those who do understand the significance of these tests could benefit from another incentive.

With part of the money that the PTSA donated to my department for tutoring sessions, we purchased prizes ranging from movie passes to gift certificates to DVD players, and we raffled them off after we received the test scores. At a class assembly, we held a drawing to recognize and celebrate those students who had passed, and we created buzz (and friendly competition) among those students who would need to take the test the following year. Offering these incentives can be crucial in helping to get students to take the tests more seriously.

Teach Test Prep.

A colleague once shared his displeasure with me for having to teach test prep to his students in order to ensure their success on a high-stakes test. He was indignant that he was being asked to help his students beat a test rather than learn material. He was right. Education should not be reduced to helping students find shortcuts. But where is the harm in teaching students how to properly take a test? We have been so conditioned to respond negatively to high-stakes testing that we are blind to the fact that we already use such practices when we prep students for AP tests and the SAT. This same teacher taught an advanced placement class, so I already knew that he was teaching his students how to break down and decode questions on the AP exam, how to use process of elimination, and other tips. Why should it be any different when it comes to barrier tests?

Teaching students information and skills necessary for success is not all there is to high-stakes testing; equipping them with as much knowledge as possible about the test itself is just as important. Students need to understand that they can write in the exam booklets, how the tests are scored, and the like. Ensure that your teachers have test prep strategies at their disposal and create a handout that they can refer to or adapt for their students (Resource 28).

Create Review Guides.

Before midterms and final exams, most teachers provide their students with some kind of review sheet or packet to help them study because the test is so crucial and covers so much material. Wouldn't it make sense then to do the same for students before they take a high-stakes test? Teachers who claim that students should be keeping a notebook and use that to study with are right; however, they miss the point. Why penalize students with the risk of not graduating? Why not equip them as best as possible? Creating a review packet should not necessarily fall on your shoulders or on one teacher in particular. When my department created review guides, one teacher was responsible for pulling together the information, but we all met to determine what should be included.

Provide Food.

Food facilitates morale for students too. As the saying goes, breakfast is the most important meal of the day. Unfortunately, many students do not get the brain food they need in the morning, either because it is not available at home or because they do not take the time to eat. Try to secure money to provide students with snacks, such as juice and bagels, on the morning of the test to ensure that they are as well armed as they can be. Because high-stakes tests are equally a test of stamina as they are of knowledge, I encourage my students to bring a small candy bar or something else to nibble on during test breaks in the hall. This way, they can get an extra boost if they are beginning to feel fatigued.

Coordinate Testing.

Although most schools have a guidance counselor or administrator solely in charge of setting up the testing schedule, a strong instructional leader will make sure that she is also involved in this process. Because teachers are the ones who proctor standardized tests, they are the ones who have the best insight into what works and what doesn't work regarding the testing process. Ask to help assign proctors and to designate testing areas.

During the actual administration, make yourself available to give your teachers breaks, to answer their questions, and to handle unexpected situations that come up. Observe the overall testing process to see what changes might be needed for the next round. For example, were hallways secure and quiet during testing? Were PA announcements made or did the bells accidentally ring at the end of the regular period thereby disrupting testing? Did the teachers who weren't proctoring a test or covering a class assist in some way? Were there alternates in place in case a proctor was absent? Was someone available to relieve proctors? Should the bell schedule have been adjusted for time lost to testing? Should students have had an extended break after testing before heading to their next period? Did proctors have extra pencils or other supplies for students who arrived unprepared to the testing site? Was there a holding site for students who came to school late? Was there a spillover site for students who needed additional time? Was someone in charge of making sure that students with individualized education programs had their needs met? Was there someone available to escort students to the bathroom or water fountain? Paying attention to these issues will help ensure that the testing process goes smoothly, creating an atmosphere for success.

Data Analysis

With such awesome technological power at our fingertips, the nature of education has changed drastically in the past few years. Specifically, technology allows us to sort and analyze data in a variety of ways that was hitherto cumbersome and often ignored. By knowing how to interpret and use data to improve your instructional program, you can become a stronger instructional leader. Although you should consider creating data-tracking sheets for your department (Resource 29), it is not possible to explain here how data can specifically be analyzed because there are different programs available that disaggregate standardized test scores. The important thing to understand is that test results must be more than entries in a grade book: they must be opportunities for discussion and means to improve instruction and achievement.

This view is shared by Paul Farmer, the principal of Kilmer Middle School in Fairfax County, Virginia. He has worked as an administrator in three different buildings in two school systems over the course of his career and has made numerous presentations about data analysis. He conducts in-house training to help teachers and administrators analyze and interpret test data and become more comfortable with using data. Farmer and I recently discussed the process of using data and what he expects from his teacher leaders. (See Resource 30 for transcript of full interview.)

Team leaders at Kilmer Middle School receive data from their administrators in the form of grade reports and high-stakes test results. They reflect on the data individually and then share with their departments, discussing obstacles, comparing scores and grades, and assessing strengths and weaknesses in the department. They also use the data to measure their class grades and averages against their standardized test scores. For example, teachers with a high number of students earning *A*s should likewise see high-stakes test scores in the advanced range.

If this is not the case, it can indicate that there is a problem and provide essential information about what is and is not working in a classroom and what a teacher is actually teaching. Such discrepancies might indicate that students are getting damaged. "Students see that they are working really hard but aren't achieving by the teacher's measure, although they are by the state's measure," says Farmer. "That can really turn off a student's drive and desire for education."

Although data won't determine how effective a given teacher is, data can pave the way for change. According to Farmer, data allow you to start a dialogue, one based on fact not on opinion or observation. Data help identify goals and measure progress. The objective is data-driven instruction, which Farmer defines as "the use of student data and analysis of these data to make instructional decisions to change or maintain the habit of instruction or the current instructional methods. The data are either going to say that 'yes, this is good,' or that something needs to be addressed." Consequently, teachers shouldn't be married to a particular methodology because it's fashionable or because they like it; they need to understand and respond to what the data indicate.

Some teachers may react negatively to using data, so you should encourage them to view it as an opportunity for professional growth. After reflecting on the data, don't tell your teachers what needs to be done; rather, ask them what they think the data show and solicit suggestions on ways to improve. If instructional modifications are warranted, offer to help in any way you can. Your focus should not be on what someone did wrong but on assisting your teachers in identifying and helping those students who need it. And be sure to inform your administrator about the process because you'll require his support to effect change. Simply gathering data, or identifying successes and failures, is not enough. You need to look for patterns and discuss them with your administrator, department, and individual teachers.

Train your teachers to look at data and, as a team, analyze and interpret results.

The goal is to turn data into meaningful information that will improve or enhance instruction and achievement on your team. For example, have your team conduct an item analysis on a test or a midterm where you determine how many students missed each question (information that Scantron machines can produce) and discuss the areas in which students succeeded and failed. Is your team surprised that a large number of students answered a certain question incorrectly? After determining which questions were most often missed, assess the validity of the questions. Were they faulty questions, were the answers ambiguous, or did a typo change the meaning? If these problems did not exist, then is the high rate of failure particular to a certain teacher, class, or the entire grade level? Regardless of which one of the three is the answer, what is your GoalAction to remedy the situation?

Encourage your teachers to share their results across the grade level or like subjects. This kind of discussion can be beneficial because perhaps someone's class fared better in areas than others' classes. Of course, the next logical question is, why is that? Is it solely because of students' ability levels? Or is someone doing something different, or better, than everyone else? Have your teachers use this as an opportunity to collaborate and share strategies that will benefit all teachers and students in the department. Then take this a step further by having all the grade level leaders meet for a vertical discussion based on the results. The 9th grade team leader can share with the 10th grade leader what the general trends are, and so on, to better prepare the receiving teachers on what to expect, and they in turn might be able to offer ideas or strategies that can be used as interventions in the meantime.

Afterword

Inviting teachers to participate in the decision-making process by elevating them to leadership roles should be viewed as a means to accomplish significant change in the field of education. Rethinking traditional concepts of leaders and followers or moving away from classical models of management can increase teacher motivation and improve climate. According to SERVE, an education organization that focuses on leadership and educator quality, teacher leaders can "affect student learning; contribute to school improvement; inspire excellence in practice; and empower stakeholders to participate in educational improvement" (as cited in Childs-Bowen, Moller, & Scrivner, 2000, p. 28). Therefore, schools need to nurture leadership and adequately equip their teacher leaders with the skills necessary to move education further into the 21st century.

It's true that leadership often means increased responsibility, and, consequently, increased accountability, but who better than the teacher leader to take that on? As Robert Crandall, former president and chairman of American Airlines, explains, "The ideal leader for the 21st century will be one who creates an environment that encourages everyone in the organization to stretch their capabilities and achieve a shared vision, who gives people the confidence to run farther and faster than they ever have before, and who establishes the conditions for people to be more productive, more innovative, more creative and feel more in charge of their own lives than they ever dreamed possible" (as cited in McFarland, Senn, & Childress, 1993, p. 183).

But you will certainly encounter obstacles along the way. Failure is to be expected, and at times it should be welcomed, because we generally learn more from our failures than from our successes. Disheartening as that might sound, consider this: even the legendary Joe DiMaggio struck out. The great Yankee Clipper, often regarded as one of the best hitters in baseball, got a base hit approximately one out of every three trips to the plate—hardly impressive statistics to someone unfamiliar with baseball. But succeeding only one-third of the time was impressive enough for DiMaggio to earn entry into the Hall of Fame because of the difficulty of the game and the skills needed to succeed.

Education and teacher leadership are no different. You will not succeed with every swing of the bat: leadership and improving achievement can be more difficult than hitting a hard slider off the corner of the plate. A good administrator will recognize this and grant you some latitude and support, and you should do the same with the teachers on your team. And if you are trying and taking risks to improve your program, then the more swings you take, the greater the odds that you will get a hit—or a home run.

My aim with this book is to equip, energize, and inspire teachers to take on leadership positions, including those already in leadership roles, in an attempt to improve education from within rather than allowing outside observers to dictate remedies. As educators, we have a keener insight into the strengths, as well as the ills, inherent in the field; we are also the best poised to ameliorate those shortcomings we have control over.

I also hope to give administrators a fresh perspective on the workings within their buildings; on the potential for teacher leadership to improve morale and increase student achievement; and on ways teachers can be coached to become better leaders. However, with so many administrators set to retire in the next few years, the responsibility lies with us, the teacher leaders—those who are simultaneously student, teacher, and leader and who have a vested interest to reform and to push education forward.

Yet closing the leadership gap extends even further than teacher leaders; we must instill leadership characteristics and

strategies in our students while involving them as active partici-
pants in their learning, their future. Several high schools now offer
leadership classes for students, and such efforts need to be supported, promoted, and encouraged, especially because there is
much we can learn from our students.

During exit interviews I recently conducted with my seniors as
part of their final exams, I asked them to relate the greatest lesson
they learned from holding a leadership position, formal or informal. The responses of students, a couple of whom intend to be
teachers, were very telling: "Motivating people is a large part of
leadership," "Leadership is getting people to do something they
might not want to do," "It's impossible to please everyone, especially since you have to focus on the overall good of the group,"
and "You need to be a good follower in order to be a good leader."

If we can enable more of our students and teachers to gain such
insight, then we will be well on our way toward true teacher leadership: building a better tomorrow by improving education from
within.

References

Childs-Bowen, D., Moller, G., & Scrivner, J. (2000, May). Principals: Leaders of
leaders. *NASSP Bulletin, 84*(616), 27–34.

McFarland, L. J., Senn, L. E., & Childress, J. R. (1993). *21st century leadership:
Dialogues with 100 top leaders*. Los Angeles, CA: Leadership Press.

RESOURCES

RESOURCE 1
A Checklist for Mentors

Getting your new teachers off on the right foot is an essential part of helping them and you succeed. There are many things that a new teacher or a teacher new to your building needs to know before school starts and during the first few weeks. Although this is not an exhaustive list, it should give you an idea of the things that you or a mentor should keep in mind.

I have . . .

_____ obtained the new teacher's contact information and given him mine.

_____ given him an informational packet on classroom management, unit and lesson planning, and assessments.

_____ helped him create the most effective room setup.

_____ talked with him about homework, late work, grading, and attendance policies.

_____ provided him with copies of the state and local standards.

_____ made him aware of Web sites that support learning objectives.

_____ provided him with sample syllabi and course overviews.

_____ given him an example of a greeting letter to parents.

_____ given him an example of a student information sheet or questionnaire.

_____ given him instructional supplies and explained how to obtain them in the future.

_____ shown him where ancillary materials are located.

_____ given him the copier code.

_____ introduced him to essential personnel.

_____ explained how to call in an absence.

_____ discussed fire drill and crisis procedures with him.

_____ shown him where to get information regarding school delays and closings.

_____ emphasized the importance of creating three days of emergency lesson plans.

_____ paired him with a team partner in case he misses a meeting.

_____ given him a copy of a failure/tardy/absence form letter.

_____ spoken with him about the importance of being firm yet fair with students early in the year.

_____ discussed his disciplinary plan with him.

_____ stressed the importance of having an engaging lesson on the first day of school instead of simply going over rules and policies.

_____ given him an example of a classroom survey so that he can get feedback from his students.

_____ secured him his own classroom; if he floats, I have provided him with a cart, extra materials, or some kind of privilege to make the situation more palatable.

_____ spoken with him about what to do and say and what not to do and say on Back-to-School Night and given him a parent information sheet for that evening.

_____ reviewed a system for documenting situations concerning students.

_____ discussed setting goals that we will review at the semester break.

_____ set aside time during the first month of school and subsequent teacher workdays to touch base with him.

_____ modeled professional behavior through my interactions with colleagues, bell-to-bell instruction, valid assessments, timely return of assignments, and a positive yet honest, realistic attitude.

Create a warm and inviting atmosphere for students visiting your school for field experience. Welcoming student teachers aboard exhibits professionalism and can help them feel as though they are part of the team.

August 20, 2003

Ms. Sarah Daniels
2501 William Street
Fairfax, VA 20151

Dear Sarah:

Thank you for your interest in Kennedy High School!

Teachers report to work by 7:05 a.m. and the contract day ends at 2:35 p.m. Although your course requirements might not dictate that you log a full day, you might find it educational to do so once or twice during your field experience to get a feel for a full day with students.

We offer a variety of classes, so please let me know what you are most interested in observing (i.e., if you would like to see an accelerated class, a remedial class, a team-taught class, a particular grade level or type of instruction).

Finally, please let me know what your course requirements are and what is expected of the host teacher.

I look forward to hearing from you,

John Gabriel

RESOURCE 3
Student Teacher Schedule

You might follow up on your initial letter by sending your student teacher a schedule that you have created based on his or her course requirements.

September 8, 2003

Ms. Sarah Daniels
2501 William Street
Fairfax, VA 20151

Dear Sarah:

I have planned a schedule for you for Wednesday, October 22, and Thursday, October 23 (see below). I will meet you in the main office at 7:05 a.m. and give you a map and bell schedule at that time. We have a refrigerator and a microwave in our workroom, so you can bring a lunch if you'd like. At the end of these two days we will talk to plan your further observations.

See you Wednesday!

John Gabriel

Observation schedule for Sarah Daniels:

Wednesday, October 22

Period	Time	Teacher	Course	Room #
1	7:20–9:05 a.m.	Laura Fitzgerald	AP English	240
3	9:20–11:00 a.m.	John Smith	English 11	243
5	11:10 a.m.–12:00 p.m.	Karinne Henley and Matt Coles	English 9 Teamed	245
7	12:40–2:10 p.m.	Sue Stanton	Developmental Reading	238

Thursday, October 23

Period	Time	Teacher	Course	Room #
2	7:20–9:05 a.m.	Kim Davis	English 9 Honors	242
4	9:20–11:00 a.m.	Josh Carter	English 10	243
5	11:10 a.m.–12:00 p.m.	Becky Rivera	Transitional English	246
6	12:40–2:10 p.m.	Chris Winters and Diana Long	English 12 Teamed	244

RESOURCE 4
Practicum Survey

Reflection is an essential component of growth. After host teachers complete evaluations of their practicum students, they should give them brief surveys in order to improve the experience for future students.

1. Was your stay at Kennedy High School a positive experience? Why or why not?

2. What would have improved your time at Kennedy High School?

3. What do you wish you could have seen more of?

4. Please explain why your experience with your host teacher was a positive or negative one.

5. Was your host teacher responsive or unresponsive to your needs? How?

6. Was your host teacher available if needed?

7. Did your host teacher provide you with significant and meaningful feedback?

8. How could your host teacher have better served you?

9. What did you like the most about your time at Kennedy High School? What did you like the least?

10. Would you recommend Kennedy High School to your peers who are seeking to complete their field experience? Why or why not?

Additional comments:

RESOURCE 5
Content-Based Interview Questions

The following sample content-based interview questions can be easily adapted for almost any grade level. The questions here are by no means comprehensive, so add to them or create your own versions of them as needed.

Science Questions

Biology

- What are some activities you have used to teach genetics and heredity?

- What are your thoughts about teaching evolution?

- What kinds of lab activities would you incorporate in a unit on cell division, or animal life cycles, or parts of a flower?

- How do you teach a difficult concept such as cell respiration?

Physics

- What do you do for students having difficulties with the math concepts associated with physics?

- What are students' misconceptions about the earth/sun/moon system and how do you overcome them?

- How do you feel about using technology to teach lessons on motion and forces?

Chemistry

- What are some ways you help students understand the periodic table?

- How can you connect ideas such as atomic structure or chemical reactions to things students already know?

- Can you think of a lab that helps students understand Charles' law, or Boyle's law, or the difference between heat and temperature?

Geology

- How do you make the rock cycle interesting to students?

- What are some ways of incorporating the local environment into your teaching?

- How do you teach or enable students to comprehend theoretical concepts such as plate tectonics?

Foreign Language Questions

- What types of strategies or activities do you use to teach vocabulary?

- What strategies do you use to promote oral proficiency?

- What do you do for students who have difficulty in grasping grammar?

- How do you incorporate the use of multiple intelligences in teaching foreign language?

- It is not uncommon to have LD students in a foreign language classroom, but foreign language classes are not usually teamed classes. How do you meet these students' needs?

- Do you incorporate target language reading into the curriculum? If so, how?

- What role does culture play in the foreign language classroom?

- How do you help students develop proficiency in writing?

ESOL Questions

- What general language acquisition theories do you subscribe to? Why?

- With so many different levels of language proficiency in the ESOL (English for speakers of other languages) classroom, how do you reach all your students?

- How do you use language-learning skills (reading, writing, listening, and speaking) in your class?

- How do you assess for understanding, mastery, and fluency in the language-learning classroom?

- What role do world cultures play in the language-learning classroom?

- Do you believe that an ESOL teacher should teach students new to a culture about its acceptable behavior? If so, how?

- With the potential for so many different cultures in the classroom, how do you ensure that students do not feel intimidated by cultures other than their own?

English Questions

- What strategies do you use to teach the writing process?

- How do you improve a student's writing?

- How do you organize and teach the research paper or research unit?

- How do you teach literary analysis or help students understand abstract or difficult concepts such as symbolism, theme, or an author's writing style?

- Studying grammar is often a dry lesson—are there any creative approaches for teaching it?

- English teachers have traditionally not seen themselves as reading teachers. What reading strategies do you have at your disposal?

- With so many students who are nonreaders, how do you make the English classroom relevant to their lives?

- How do you determine what vocabulary to study? What strategies or activities do you use to teach it?

Math Questions

- How do you feel about calculators and technology being used in a math classroom?

- Are there benefits to students using graphing calculators in Algebra? Drawbacks?

- As you are working out a problem, a student points out a mistake that you've made. How do you respond or handle it?

- Is there a purpose to homework in a math classroom? Explain.

- Do students learn math concepts best by traditional methods (notes, practice, homework) or by alternative methods (projects, competitions, group problem solving)? Explain.

- Do you believe that a student can learn mathematics by playing games? Why or why not?

- How would you relate concepts learned while studying linear equations to the study of quadratic equations?

- How do you relate math to your students' lives?

Social Studies Questions

- Why is it important to study history?
- Do you teach students citizenship or how to be productive members of society? If so, how?
- What would your approach be toward teaching a certain time period or geographical region?
- Do you use primary resources in your class? Why or why not? If so, how?
- How do you help students see history as something interesting instead of just a collection of dates and places?
- Give an example of cultural diffusion.
- How do you show the influence and effect of past civilizations on present ones?
- What historical trends do you highlight and how do you convey them?
- What role and influence has religion had on the development of civilizations?
- How might you incorporate economics in the curriculum?

RESOURCE 6
Keeping It Together

With all that must be done in and out of the classroom during the school day, it is very easy to forget little things (sometimes even the big things!). This form can be included in a plan book to help us remember when we assigned work (which is invaluable for a parent conference) and what we have yet to do (send home an individualized progress report, e.g.), as well as to keep track of the innumerable "promises" we make with students (such as agreeing to bring in money for a fundraiser, having make-up work ready, and the like).

Week of _____

I told _____ period on _____ to have _____

_____ by _____.

Notes/promises:

. . . .

I told _____ period on _____ to have _____

_____ by _____.

Notes/promises:

. . . .

I told _____ period on _____ to have _____

_____ by _____.

Notes/promises:

. . . .

RESOURCE 7
Teacher Wish List

Wish lists not only give you an idea of what your teachers want to teach, they also can help you stay organized at staffing meetings or when you start creating the master schedule.

Although I cannot guarantee that you will receive everything you ask for, I will do my best to honor at least one request. Please complete the following as honestly as you can. Your responses will not be shared with anyone.

Name _____

I would like to teach the following:

_____   _____   _____

I am open to a teamed class (please circle):   Yes   No

If I had to team teach, I would like to team the following classes or with the following people:

_____   _____   _____

If I had to team teach, I would find it very difficult to team with the following people:

_____   _____   _____

I would prefer having my planning period during:

I would like to sponsor the following:

Is there anything else you would like me to keep in mind when creating the master schedule?

RESOURCE 8
Memo Documentation

If you have already spoken with teachers about the need to follow through on a professional responsibility and reminded them or followed up with them, then the next step might be to write a memo so they know you're going to involve your administrator.

TO: Sam Delino

FROM: John Gabriel

DATE: September 15, 2001

RE: Pre-testing

During 3rd period, I informally assessed which classes in the main English hallway were taking the department's pre-test. It appeared that your class did not have time at the beginning or end of any period this week to do so, even though this had been agreed upon at our summer inservice meeting.

Please plan to meet with me at 2:15 p.m. on Thursday, September 17, in my office so we can find a way to ensure that this pre-testing occurs in your classes.

xc: Howard Stiles, Assistant Principal

| RESOURCE 9 |
| Welcome-Back Letter |

Set the climate for the school year before it even begins. Send your teachers a welcome-back letter or letter of introduction before summer inservice meetings to share good news, to welcome new colleagues, or to relay important information.

August 1, 2003

Greetings returning and new colleagues!

It's difficult to believe that summer is nearly over. It seems that the older I get, the quicker the summer vacations become. Nevertheless, I am looking forward to coming back to school. Believe it or not, August is Admit You're Happy Month, and I admit that although I do not relish the idea of waking up again at 5:30 a.m., I am happy to be heading back into the classroom and excited about working with you this year!

The good news is that we had another year of tremendous successes ranging from our drama productions to our forensics wins, SOL tutoring program, and standardized test scores. The preliminary results for the Writing and Reading SOL tests are amazing—we have truly outdone ourselves! Hats off to the 11th grade team for shouldering the burden of work to improve test scores, but, at the same time, the gains we made should be attributed to everyone in the department.

Wednesday, August 13, is the day for our first regular department meeting, which will double as our inservice meeting. Tentative issues that we will address include the following:

- Housekeeping items
- Curriculum maps and essential questions
- Revisions to the program of studies
- Grade level meetings
- New support systems for student achievement
- Review of test scores and pertinent data
- Inventory and rearrangement of the book room

We will meet at 8:00 a.m. in room 240, and if you have suggestions for other topics, please let me know as soon as possible.

Finally, as you already know, Amy Oliver transferred at the end of the year, but as some of you might not know, Kay Johnson resigned to pursue a graduate degree full-time. So please welcome Sue Smith, who is joining us from Maryland, and Kate Cox, who comes to us from Connecticut, to our team.

I hope you are as excited as I am about the upcoming year!

Sincerely,

John Gabriel

RESOURCE 10
Letter to New Teacher Leader

Give your new teacher leader a description or outline of expectations regarding her role. Such a letter also demonstrates an atmosphere of professionalism.

July 15, 2003

Ms. Jill Marin
37 Western Way
Laurel, MD 20707

Dear Jill:

As the team leader for the 12th grade, you have the opportunity to demonstrate your leadership potential and content knowledge by helping to implement vision and provide direction for the English department. Although you might feel overwhelmed at times because of your normal responsibilities, please realize that this exceptional experience will allow you not only to assist the department with its goals but also to help Kennedy High School students, the reason we all are here.

Tentative responsibilities for this position include:

- holding team meetings;
- keeping the minutes of team meetings and submitting them to me;
- informing me of grade level needs, concerns, and situations;
- coordinating the use of books;
- leading curriculum development;
- developing remediation plans;
- providing staff development; and
- initiating action research.

I applaud your willingness to help the entire learning community and look forward to working with you throughout the year. If you have any questions or concerns, please do not hesitate to see me.

Sincerely,

John Gabriel

RESOURCE 11
E-mail Documentation

In addition to being an efficient way to communicate, e-mail can be an important tool for informal or formal documentation.

From: Gabriel, John G.
Sent: Thursday, March 13, 2003 8:45 AM
To: Winkler, Tom
Subject: Thanks!

Tom,

Just wanted to drop you a quick line to say thanks for being willing to take on the responsibility of posting information to the department's Web site. This will be a great resource for students and parents, and I'm glad you're the one who will be heading this up because no one can match your knowledge of technology.

Thanks again,
John

. . . .

From: Gabriel, John G.
Sent: Friday, October 05, 2001 1:05 PM
To: Crenshaw, Kristen; Everly, Marsha
Cc: Fielder, Tom; Showalter, Deenie
Subject: Post-conference

Thank you for taking the time to meet with us on October 4.

Although we all agreed that there were many positive things going on in your class, we were also in agreement that the structure of your review activity needed improvement in order to minimize class disruptions. As a result, we reached the following conclusions:

> flexibility is important in planning and instruction,
> a successful lesson comes out of open communication during the planning process,
> both of you are responsible for classroom management in your teamed class,
> Marsha will concentrate on increasing her volume to convey a higher degree of confidence to the students,
> mobility and proximity are essential elements to classroom management, and
> both of you will participate in the teaming inservice session on October 17.

Thank you for your willingness to discuss the state of your teamed class, and if I can be of any further help, please do not hesitate to ask.

Sincerely,
John

RESOURCE 12
Department Meeting Agenda

List agenda items in order of importance, with items that are time sensitive first. When possible, include a brief write-up underneath the agenda topic so that you don't waste time at the meeting explaining the issue. This also gives people advance notice of what to expect at the meeting, thereby allowing them time to digest the issue, ponder questions, and brainstorm solutions—important elements of successful meetings.

Because there never seem to be enough hours in the day, don't take the time to go over information in meetings that your teachers could easily read on their own. Instead, take advantage of assigned meeting time by focusing on needs and growth. Announcements and information can be included at the bottom of the agenda, and key phrases can be bolded to call attention to them and make reading them easier.

The sample agenda below, adapted from two different meetings, shows how you might incorporate these suggestions to make your meetings more productive.

Location: Room 133
Next meeting: 3/29

Instructional Council Agenda 3/9/04

1. Honor code (5 minutes)

A faculty member has asked the following: After an honor code violation, is National Honor Society notified, how is it notified, and how is this information being compiled? Bring any other related questions you might have to the meeting.

2. Instructional assistants (10 minutes)

The instructional assistants have two concerns that came out of one of their meetings: (1) should they be responsible for classroom management? and (2) how can they be more involved in lesson planning with teachers? Consider these questions and be prepared to share suggestions.

3. Exam exemptions (10 minutes)

Even though final exams are still a few months away, we need to address exemptions so that we can start promoting this among the students. How did we handle exemptions last year? Are we happy with how we handled them last year?

4. May SOL tests (15 minutes)

The testing window appears to be 5/23, 5/27–5/30, and maybe 6/1. What was the feedback from the department meetings in reference to the May SOL testing schedule? What concerns or problems did we note last year?

5. Failing students (25 minutes)

In some schools, during the first part of the year, averages of students who failed miserably for the quarter are automatically bumped up from around 20 percent to 50 percent, so that a student still has a chance of passing for the semester or year. How do people feel about this?

6. Returned work (20 minutes)

Does your department have a policy on returning tests? For example, can students keep their tests? Do students even get to see their tests or are they simply given a Scantron form back with a number on it? Are tests used as tools for reteaching?

Supplemental Information
[from Mission Possible Agenda 3/16/02]

1. Please let your **subs** know that they need to be here by **7:05 a.m.,** not when your first class starts.

2. Interim **bubble sheets** are due before Monday, **April 4.**

3. **Textbook adoption** will not occur until 2004–2005 for English, which means that we won't actually get books until **Fall '05,** if then.

4. If you are interested in making **extra money,** see me for an application to serve on **adoption committees** for textbooks and curriculum.

5. **Rising freshmen orientation** is on **4/27** from **7:00–9:00 p.m.** If you are unsure if you need to attend, see me. Displays should relate to electives that freshmen are eligible to take. The custodians will set up tables after lunch, but **you are responsible for setting up** your own equipment (TV, VCR, etc.) **and removing your display.**

6. **Guidance counselors** will be coming into classrooms to promote the next round of the SAT. They will be in classes on **3/24 & 3/25 (12th grade)** and **3/27 & 3/28 (11th grade).** I have been assured that the visits will not last longer than 10 minutes.

7. **3/30** is the **deadline** for submitting **activities and events** for next year.

8. The administration wants us to remember that **we should not send students to the attendance office if they are tardy within the first 20 minutes of class.** If it is excused, they will already have a pass. If not, it is unexcused.

RESOURCE 13
Department Meeting Minutes

After minutes have been taken, allow a brief period of time for team or depart-ment members to review them and make amendments before they become department record.

Date: 1/6/04

Present: Lauren Kelly, Nancy Bellings, Larry Smith, Sue Stanton, Chris Klein, Marie Devry, Danielle Washington, Michelle Lansing, Latisha Jones, Jorge Ramos, Peter Grafton, Bill Schmidt, Megan Yardley, Jesse Holmes, Alison Brown, Sarah Kincaid, Catherine Bowman, Ellen Marinakis, Donna Highlander, John Gabriel

Latecomers: Debbie Stein (2:25 p.m.), Gary Shaw (2:26 p.m.), Dara Klowski (2:27 p.m.)

Guests: Peter Hall

Meeting started at 2:20 p.m.

1. The March Standards of Learning test

   ▪ March 9 (Multiple Choice) and March 10 (Direct Writing)

   ▪ Teachers are responsible for creating lesson plans for displaced classes.

   ▪ Dictionaries are available on March 10 ONLY.

   ▪ Teachers should cover or remove instructional materials in classrooms and get dictionaries for testing rooms.

   ▪ There will be "holding room" for students who need additional time.

   ▪ Test proctor training is mandatory and will occur next month.

2. AP and honors recommendations

   ▪ Common writing prompts will be used for each grade level, to be com-pleted using roughly 20 minutes in class (not PAWS); it is suggested to do this during or in lieu of SSR, so as not to interrupt instruction.

   ▪ Prompts will be copied and distributed by team leaders; we will use the same prompts as last year. They should be administered the week of January 20–23, because course selections are February 4–6.

▪ The prompts are not designed to exclude or weed out, but to tap students who might be flying underneath our radar. Alison offered testimony on how this process aided in identifying two of her students for honors classes last year. It is an additional tool to help the teacher and counselor determine the best placement for every student. The score of the writing prompt is not the sole factor in determining the student's placement.

▪ Prompts circulate among two or three teachers per grade level and most likely will be scored during January 27 inservice day.

▪ Students should NOT be given guidance or help on the prompt; there should be no introductory lesson. Last year, at least two students wrote, ". . . because my teacher told me so" in their prompts.

3. Mini-lesson on poetry: Lauren Kelly

▪ Use a jigsaw technique to teach poetry, literary devices, and their effect; demonstration using Seamus Heaney's "Blackberry-Picking."

▪ E-mail Lauren for details or extra copies of lesson and handouts.

4. How do we teach vocabulary?

▪ Resources include *1100 Words You Need to Know* and other books, and a packet of prefixes/roots/suffixes, which Donna currently has.

▪ Warm-up packets to be designed, using roots; include analogies for SAT review.

▪ Be sure to incorporate the Word of the Day in class in some way.

▪ Suggestion: a collaboration meeting to write vocabulary packets together.

▪ Other suggestions: visual vocabulary (à la Sarah Kincaid).

▪ Alison will be attending a conference where there will be a session on vocabulary strategies; she will report back to us.

Meeting ended at 3:00 p.m.
Respectfully submitted by Lauren Kelly

RESOURCE 14
Identifying Effective Meetings

Although people don't necessarily always like them, rules, or common under-standings, are essential for effective meetings. The below can be used as a framework for organizing your meetings. Review these characteristics and behaviors with your team and discuss their ramifications. Or team members could brainstorm their own lists, discuss how to achieve effective behavior and avoid non-conducive behavior, and set their own ground rules. Basically, organizations (even smaller groups such as departments and teams are organizations in their own right) need some semblance of order to function competently. Improving communication will improve your meetings, as will doing some or all of the following at times: remaining neutral, being observant, talking little and listening more, asking for members' assistance, addressing problematic behavior after meetings, and even involving your administrator.

Ineffective meetings	Effective meetings
✗ Meetings start late. ✗ Meetings end late.	✓ Meetings start promptly. ✓ Meetings start at a consistent time. ✓ Meetings end at a reasonable time. ✓ Agenda items have time limits. ✓ Someone monitors time and maintains pace.
✗ Members digress from the topic at hand. ✗ Members engage in side conversations. ✗ Members engage in grading, planning, or other unrelated work.	✓ Members stay on task with the topic at hand. ✓ Members leave unrelated work at the door. ✓ Someone helps keep the group focused on agenda items.
✗ Meeting purpose is unclear.	✓ Meeting purpose is clear. ✓ Members understand the goal of the meeting.
✗ Agenda is unclear or there is no agenda. ✗ Agenda deals mainly with housekeeping or general administrative items.	✓ Agenda is clear and precise. ✓ Agenda centers on professional growth and meeting the needs of students. ✓ Members are able to add agenda items and are clear on this procedure. ✓ Agenda is distributed before meeting to team members.

Ineffective meetings	Effective meetings
✗ Members are often tardy or absent, or leave meetings early. ✗ Interruptions are frequent.	✓ Entire team is present. ✓ Set meeting times and dates enable members to block out time to prevent conflicting obligations. ✓ Members inform team ahead of time if they will be absent. ✓ Representatives attend in place of absent members.
✗ There is no record.	✓ Minutes are recorded. ✓ Minutes are reviewed and approved by all team members.
✗ Misinformation is common. ✗ Information is assumed.	✓ Minutes are disseminated. ✓ Information is explicit.
✗ Members are not prepared.	✓ Members arrive prepared and ready to work.
✗ Roles are unclear.	✓ Members have clear, formal roles or take on informal leadership roles. ✓ Expectations are clearly illustrated.
✗ Members don't listen to one another. ✗ Members cut each other off.	✓ Members exhibit attentiveness to colleagues and don't talk until speakers have finished their points. ✓ Members clarify, paraphrase, and rephrase what is being discussed.
✗ Members monopolize time or the floor.	✓ All voices and opinions are encouraged. ✓ Talk time is monitored.
✗ Agenda pushing is present.	✓ Members serve the students' best interests.
✗ Members are committed to self.	✓ Members are committed first to cause and then to one another and to achieving excellence.
✗ Inability to agree turns to rancor.	✓ Opposing viewpoints are welcomed, weighed, and discussed in a professional manner with the understanding that the final decision is not about teachers but about students. ✓ Process for achieving agreement and consensus is clear.
✗ Negativity dominates meetings.	✓ Positive climate is established through professional leadership.

RESOURCE 15
GoalAction Sheet

Identify your areas of need in order to determine your goals and the subsequent actions you should take to achieve them. This can help you stay focused during and outside of team meetings and keep everyone on the same page.

Area of focus	Goal	Deadline	Evidence of need for goal	Contact person	Team members	Strategy	Assessment dates/results

RESOURCE 16
Status Sheet

A status sheet, which sometimes can take the place of minutes, can help update administrators, keep team members in the loop, and provide documentation on your progress toward a goal.

Area of focus	Goal	Contact person	Team members	Obstacles	Method of circumvention	Needs	Next assessment date

RESOURCE 17
Conflict Resolution Survey

Conflict resolution can be an ugly and tedious process. To facilitate mediation between both parties, ask each person to complete the following prior to meeting with them. This will allow them to organize their thoughts rather than speak rashly and, as a result, regret something that they might say. This will also give you the opportunity to further analyze the situation before the conference.

How do you think a teamed class should function? What is your ideal teaming situation?

What are the three main problems in your teamed class?

1.

2.

3.

List three parts of your partner's role or three things that you believe he should be doing:

1.

2.

3.

List three parts of your role:

1.

2.

3.

List three things that would improve your teaming environment:

1.

2.

3.

RESOURCE 18
Teamed Goal Agreement

At the end of a meeting, have the disputing parties complete the following together (or separately) to cement their plan to resolve the situation and to help them stay focused after the meeting.

Our goals to improve our teamed situation are the following:

1.

2.

3.

To facilitate achieving these goals, I will do the following:

1.

2.

3.

RESOURCE 19
Collaboration and Climate Survey

This survey focuses on grade level teams, their leadership, and the ability to work together (similar to the survey that follows). After tallying the responses, share the data and discuss the surveys with your team.

1. My team leader provides us with an agenda in a timely fashion.

Strongly agree	Agree	Do not know	Disagree	Strongly disagree
1	2	3	4	5

2. My team leader adheres to the agenda and minimizes digressions.

Strongly agree	Agree	Do not know	Disagree	Strongly disagree
1	2	3	4	5

3. Our reason for meeting is clear and understood by all.

Strongly agree	Agree	Do not know	Disagree	Strongly disagree
1	2	3	4	5

4. We discuss instructional strategies and best practices at our meetings.

Strongly agree	Agree	Do not know	Disagree	Strongly disagree
1	2	3	4	5

5. We share successful lessons, activities, and assessments at our meetings.

Strongly agree	Agree	Do not know	Disagree	Strongly disagree
1	2	3	4	5

6. We analyze data at our meetings to determine areas for improvement.

Strongly agree	Agree	Do not know	Disagree	Strongly disagree
1	2	3	4	5

7. We develop GoalActions in a collaborative manner to address areas needing improvement.

Strongly agree	Agree	Do not know	Disagree	Strongly disagree
1	2	3	4	5

8. We are effective collaborators.

Strongly agree	Agree	Do not know	Disagree	Strongly disagree
1	2	3	4	5

9. My team leader provides us with staff development or literature pertinent to curricular needs.

Strongly agree	Agree	Do not know	Disagree	Strongly disagree
1	2	3	4	5

10. Everyone has the opportunity to contribute during our meetings.

Strongly agree	Agree	Do not know	Disagree	Strongly disagree
1	2	3	4	5

11. Everyone has the opportunity to participate in decision making.

Strongly agree	Agree	Do not know	Disagree	Strongly disagree
1	2	3	4	5

12. When appropriate, my team leader attempts to achieve consensus.

Strongly agree	Agree	Do not know	Disagree	Strongly disagree
1	2	3	4	5

13. Tasks and responsibilities are shared by all.

Strongly agree	Agree	Do not know	Disagree	Strongly disagree
1	2	3	4	5

14. Meetings start promptly and conclude in the allotted time.

Strongly agree	Agree	Do not know	Disagree	Strongly disagree
1	2	3	4	5

RESOURCE 20
Leadership and Climate Survey

Ask your team to evaluate your leadership and give members an opportunity to assess the department's progress toward achieving its goals. Reflect on the responses, share the data with your team, and refine your practices.

With your help, I hope to improve how I serve you as well as how we function as a team. You need not put your name on the survey, and comments can be made on the back. Completed surveys can be left in my in-box.

1. We keep a good pace at department meetings.

Strongly agree	Agree	Do not know	Disagree	Strongly disagree
1	2	3	4	5

2. We digress too much during discussions.

Strongly agree	Agree	Do not know	Disagree	Strongly disagree
1	2	3	4	5

3. Team meetings are productive.

Strongly agree	Agree	Do not know	Disagree	Strongly disagree
1	2	3	4	5

4. Department meetings are productive.

Strongly agree	Agree	Do not know	Disagree	Strongly disagree
1	2	3	4	5

5. My voice is heard at meetings.

Strongly agree	Agree	Do not know	Disagree	Strongly disagree
1	2	3	4	5

6. My voice is heard when I meet with my chair.

Strongly agree	Agree	Do not know	Disagree	Strongly disagree
1	2	3	4	5

7. My chair has been responsive to my concerns and issues.

Strongly agree	Agree	Do not know	Disagree	Strongly disagree
1	2	3	4	5

8. I have felt supported by my chair.

| Strongly agree | Agree | Do not know | Disagree | Strongly disagree |
| 1 | 2 | 3 | 4 | 5 |

9. I have been provided with materials, instructional strategies, or professional literature that has benefited me.

| Strongly agree | Agree | Do not know | Disagree | Strongly disagree |
| 1 | 2 | 3 | 4 | 5 |

10. Communication is clear, helpful, and timely.

| Strongly agree | Agree | Do not know | Disagree | Strongly disagree |
| 1 | 2 | 3 | 4 | 5 |

11. My chair handles conflict and other issues in a professional and effective manner.

| Strongly agree | Agree | Do not know | Disagree | Strongly disagree |
| 1 | 2 | 3 | 4 | 5 |

12. My chair celebrates our successes and recognizes individual achievement.

| Strongly agree | Agree | Do not know | Disagree | Strongly disagree |
| 1 | 2 | 3 | 4 | 5 |

13. The department is aware of its goals, agrees on its standards, and is moving in the right direction.

| Strongly agree | Agree | Do not know | Disagree | Strongly disagree |
| 1 | 2 | 3 | 4 | 5 |

14. My chair provides opportunities for professional growth.

| Strongly agree | Agree | Do not know | Disagree | Strongly disagree |
| 1 | 2 | 3 | 4 | 5 |

15. My chair provides me with and obtains instructional supplies.

| Strongly agree | Agree | Do not know | Disagree | Strongly disagree |
| 1 | 2 | 3 | 4 | 5 |

RESOURCE 21
Department Newsletter

A newsletter can be another way to improve communication and morale in your department. You can use it to recap information from meetings, to list important dates and events, to pass along announcements, and even to provide staff development and share ideas.

English NEWS

March 4, 2003

Dear Department,

**"He that outlives this day and comes safe home
Will stand a-tiptoe when this day is named . . .
We few, we happy few, we band of brothers.
For he today that sheds his blood with me
Shall be my brother."**

—William Shakespeare, *King Henry V,*
St. Crispin's Day speech

We begin our march toward the first round of SOL testing armed with a powerful arsenal: study packets, SOL review sessions, Test Pak information, and most important, department unity and a commitment to excellence. This unity and commitment helped us capture the SOL prize money for the month of January, which in turn helped us better equip the students for the Standards of Learning. We continue to fight the good fight, and it is heartening to see that no one has relented; no one has surrendered to fatigue, hopelessness, or apathy. We are in the trenches, and we are "making more than a difference." Sometimes that difference is neither readily apparent nor quantifiable, but we must remain confident that we are teaching essential skills and knowledge that will ensure success even beyond the Standards of Learning.

Our students have noticed our efforts and commitment over the past year and a half. Cognizant of a past context, the upperclassmen especially have commented on the talent in the department, the extra time we spend after school, the positive change in instruction and learning, and the departmental stability that is now present. Because they realize this, I am confident they will not let us down: they will meet the challenge of the SOL tests.

Rock on!
John

Important Dates

03/04—Faculty meeting
03/05—PTSA meeting
03/06—Heritage Night
03/11—English SOL: Multiple Choice
03/12—English SOL: Direct Writing
03/13—Touch Base with Teachers
03/14—SOL make-up tests
03/18—Department meeting
03/21—End of quarter

Congratulations!

Congrats to Sarah on her engagement!

Thank You

• Thank you, Ron, for pulling together the final revisions for the study packets for the Writing test!

• Thanks to everyone for your cooperation, patience, and willingness to pitch in when coverage was needed because of poor road conditions!

A Reminder . . .

• There are still some tasks that Karen needs our assistance with for SOL tutoring. The material is already laid out, so all you need to do is show up for an hour after school during one of the open slots.

• Review the SOL Reading packet so we can begin making additions/deletions at our next department meeting.

• Please lend Ron a helping hand and a voice of encouragement as he nears his deadline for publication of the literary magazine.

• Start tracking down student debt so that students and parents alike are not shocked when they receive considerable bills in May.

• We just received two more sets of the SOL workbooks.

Idea Swap

• At our January inservice meeting, Casey talked about publishing, about making our students' work meaningful. I ran with that and wrote an album review for the school paper so my students could see the importance of diction, sentence variety, imagery, and the like in a real-world setting. I encourage you to do something similar. Science students see their teacher conduct experiments; foods students watch their teacher prepare dinners. Very rarely do our students get to see us demonstrate our discipline in that kind of manner.

• We just finished the trial of the century (the 19th century, that is): *People v. Nora Helmer.* Her crime? Child abandonment. Trying a literary character can be done on any grade level and with any ability level, but prep time will vary. Students are pushed to think analytically and creatively while they demonstrate their knowledge of plot, characters, and theme. See me if you would like more information on how to set up a trial in your class.

'Tis the Season

Tax season is upon us. As usual, there have been changes to the tax laws, and at least two in particular affect us: lifetime educational credits and declaring up to $250 on classroom expenditures without itemization. I am nowhere near being an expert on this, but Stan has an informative article if you are interested.

Web Sites of Interest

www.grantshotline.com
Info on different groups and money out there

www.oprah.com
She has been known to give money to educators!

www.pen.k12.va.us/VDOE/Instruction/sol.html
Teaching and learning in the context of the SOL tests

Now Playing

I recently saw *Thirteen* at Shirlington (a theater that mainly carries art flicks). Written by one of the co-stars when she was 13, the film centers on a young girl who immediately discovers the overwhelming desire to fit in, to be cool, when one of her classmates makes fun of her socks. The movie explores what it means to be 13 and bombarded by a culture obsessed with youth and rooted in materialism—the lengths that adolescents go through to be accepted. However, be forewarned: the movie is very disturbing and powerful.

"Fair is foul and foul is fair."

Nope, I'm not talking baseball (although opening day is less than a month away); I'm tellin' ya *Macbeth* is coming! Push those tix till Birnam Wood comes to Dunsinane!

I have a prize for the first person who can identify the Soothsayer's response when Caesar points out that the Ides of March have come!

RESOURCE 22
Observation Memo

If you plan to write up an observation, be sure to keep detailed notes when you observe the class. In your memo, make sure you use objective language and comment on observable behavior and activity.

TO: Gregg Maloney

FROM: John Gabriel

DATE: October 20, 2001

RE: Observation and post-observation conference

I entered your team-taught English 9 class at 7:20 a.m. on October 12, 2001.

Expectations were clearly communicated. The daily agenda was displayed on the television monitor and homework assignments and reminders were posted on the blackboard. In addition, there was a bin in the front of the room for each class period where students were able to obtain extra copies of hand-outs. Before the bell rang, and without direction, students were already working on the vocabulary warm-up on the overhead. You related the curriculum to students in a meaningful manner by placing vocabulary words in a context that drew on literature and by using examples that pertained to students' lives. Students seemed familiar with the routine for working on vocabulary and with the routines of the classroom.

You maintained the momentum of instruction by transitioning to a discussion about the writing process at 7:40 a.m. To ensure success with writing, you used two important techniques. First, by asking students to respond orally to the questions "What went through your head while writing" and "What were your thoughts on the structure," you not only encouraged students to engage in reflection, but you modeled this practice as well. Second, you assisted them in organizing their writing by showing them a graphic organizer, an "X" that reinforced the structure of a successful essay.

Finally, a positive learning environment has been established; your use of humor minimized disruptions and your enthusiasm engaged students. When necessary, you used proximity to keep students on task.

During our post-observation conference, you shared that your goal for the remainder of the year is to find other ways to reach all your students and that you plan to attend a seminar on this subject.

I hope you found our conference beneficial. If there is any way I can assist you, please do not hesitate to see me.

RESOURCE 23
Curriculum Map

*A curriculum map is a powerful tool for implementing standards in your depart-
ment and on your team. Such a guide is essential to improving achievement
because it attempts to ensure that all students are learning the same skills, concepts, and materials on a grade level, which then helps to align the curriculum
vertically as well. Although it isn't necessary, the 11th grade team leader at Falls
Church High School (FCHS) thought it was helpful to include an introduction
and an explanation of the map's purpose and how it could be used.*

11th Grade Curriculum Map
Falls Church High School 2003–2004

The Map in Use

The map aligns the FCHS program of studies (POS) with the Standards of
Learning (SOL) tests, and guides teachers in designing their units and lessons
through essential questions and indicators. The map offers several options for
content, assessment strategies, and extension activities to accompany a unit.
Teachers have the freedom and flexibility in choosing content from the POS as
well as deciding what form of instruction, assessment, and extension activities
should be used. The time frame indicated for each unit should serve as a
guide; in order to complete the course of study, teachers should generally find
that their program falls within a few weeks of the map. Additionally, although
certain skills are taught throughout the year, each unit suggests specific skills
(which build in complexity and target appropriate SOL tests) that may need to
be emphasized, depending on diagnostic testing of each class.

Introductory Unit

In order to prepare students for a year of American literature and for the challenges of the SOL-based curriculum, the first two to three weeks of the year
are devoted to (1) diagnostic testing, (2) acclimation of students to the classroom, and (3) an overarching introduction to American literature.

To address the third area, teachers should select one representative text
from each of the literary periods and, in conjunction with a brief "highlight" of
each period, allow students to work in differentiated groups to extract the relevant elements of each period from that text. Teachers can select their own
texts or can work from the suggested list below:

  Puritans/Age of Faith: selections from *Of Plymouth Plantation* by William
  Bradford

- Revolutionary Era/Age of Reason: selections from *Autobiography* by Benjamin Franklin

- Romanticism: children's book version of "Rip Van Winkle," or "The Raven" or "Annabel Lee" by Edgar Allan Poe

- Transcendentalism: selections from "Nature" by Ralph Waldo Emerson

- Realism: poetry by Stephen Crane or "The Genuine Mexican Plug" by Mark Twain

- Modernism: selections from "Winter Dreams" by F. Scott Fitzgerald or "Richard Cory" by Edwin Arlington Robinson

The goals of this introductory unit are to encourage students to get to know one another and work productively together in interdependent groups (even, perhaps, in jigsaw groups), to introduce the basic elements and historical background of each literary period, to provide the context and establish an interest for the year's literary study, and to allow the teacher to diagnose students' reading abilities. One potential assessment would be for each group to create a complete poster, including key words, for a literary period. The posters could be hung in the classroom and used as guiding tools as the year progresses.

SOL objectives covered in the introductory unit:

- SOL 11.1: The student will make informative and persuasive presentations.

- SOL 11.2: The student will analyze and evaluate informative and persuasive presentations.

- SOL 11.3: The student will read and analyze relationships among American literature, history, and culture.

- SOL 11.5: The student will read and critique a variety of poetry.

Sustained Silent Reading

Sustained Silent Reading is an integral part of our English curriculum.

SOL Writing Prompts

Teachers should administer at a minimum one graded writing prompt per quarter. The prompts should be assessed using the SOL 12-point rubric used by the state of Virginia. Please see the following page for an outline of a writing prompt workshop.

SOL Writing Prompt Workshop

Objectives:

▓ **SOL 11.7:** The student will write in a variety of forms [narrative, descriptive, expository, and persuasive].
▓ **SOL 11.8:** The student will edit for correct grammar, capitalization, punctuation, spelling, sentence structure, and paragraphing.

The student will be able to:

▓ Compose a structured five-paragraph prompt response in first person.
▓ Arrange ideas into appropriate organizational patterns for multi-paragraph writing.
▓ Use transitions both within and between paragraphs.
▓ Compose a thesis statement that guides the entire response.
▓ Use phrases and clauses to extend sentence context and detail.
▓ Edit for correct internal punctuation, capitalization, parallel structure, subject-verb agreement.
▓ Vary sentence structure using compound and complex sentences.
▓ Vary and revise word order and syntax.
▓ Edit and revise work to reflect growing skill as a writer.

Stages of Writing Workshop:

1. Familiarization with the SOL 12-point writing rubric
2. Review and assessment of sample student writing (provided through NCS Mentor)
3. Types of writing: narration, exposition (including comparison/contrast and causal analysis), persuasion, and description
4. Thesis writing
5. How to construct an introduction
6. Paragraph organization: patterns and options
7. Transitions: within and between paragraphs
8. How to construct a conclusion
9. How to peer edit
10. How to revise

Notes:

This SOL writing prompt workshop can take place as its own independent unit, or can be meshed with a separate unit of study, ideally one that does not require a great deal of independent reading outside of class.

Students should have the opportunity to plan and write several SOL writing prompts during this course of study, focusing on one or more aspects of the writing process. Examples of past SOL writing prompts are available for review.

Unit 1—Puritan Writing: The Foundations of American Culture
September/October

- SOL 11.3: The student will read and analyze relationships among American literature, history, and culture.
- SOL 11.5: The student will read and critique a variety of poetry.
- SOL 11.6: The student will read and critique a variety of dramatic selections.
- SOL 11.7: The student will write in a variety of forms, with an emphasis on persuasion.
- SOL 11.8: The student will edit for correct grammar, capitalization, punctuation, spelling, sentence structure, and paragraphing.

Skills Focus—Grammar/Mechanics:

- Recognizing sentence structure, run-ons, fragments, conjunctions
- Editing for internal punctuation
- Editing for correct capitalization

Essential Questions	Indicators	County Benchmark	Content	Extension Activities	Assessments
Why did the Puritans use the written word?	Identify the forms of writing used by the Puritans.	11.1.3.a, b. 11.2.1.a. 11.5.3.c.	*Of Plymouth Plantation*	Language study: plain style versus high style	Grammar, vocabulary worksheets, quiz, in connection to language study
What cultural expectations does Puritan literature convey?	Define Puritan cultural expectations and identify them in literature.	11.2.1.a., b., c. 11.2.2.a., b. 11.5.1.a., b. 11.5.2.a., b., c.	*Journal of Madam Knight*	Language study: archaic language	Journal as personal narrative, "character analysis," group work: Plymouth charter (laws)

How did the Puritans view "their" America? Why is this the beginning of the American dream as we know it?	Define the American dream and identify the roots of it in Puritan culture and writing.	11.2.1.a., b., c. 11.2.2.a., b. 11.5.1.a., b. 11.5.2.a., b., c.	*Sinners in the Hands of an Angry God*	Describe your (or your family's) "American" immigrant experience (ancestral or personal).	Oral presentation, reading journals, writing prompt, quiz on literary elements used in speech
How did the Puritans use poetry as a tool to teach their views?	Identify parable, iambic pentameter, conceit, and other literary devices in poetry. Explain the use of poetry as a tool in teaching Puritan theology.	11.2.1.a. 11.5.1.a., b., c. 11.5.2.a., b., c.	"Some Verses upon the Burning of Our House" "Upon a Spider Catching a Fly"	Use of poetry as parable	Writing poetry, quiz on literary terms, exit slips, acting out poem, "character analysis" (Bradstreet)
Why has Puritan culture been the subject of authors throughout the various ages?	Draw connections between Puritan culture and 20th century America by reading dramatic selections critically.	11.5.1.a., b., d. 11.5.2.a., b., c.	*The Crucible*	Language study, connection to McCarthyism of 1950s	Unit test, comparison/contrast, character bone study, plot summary
How can narrative writing be used to express our own experience with the American dream?	Use narrative writing as a tool to express oneself.	Standards 1, 2, 3	Narrative writing (in connection with Sarah Kemble Knight, Mary Rowlandson, William Bradford, and other Puritan writers)		Journal writing (pre-writing), narrative writing paper in relationship to American dream

RESOURCE 24
Student Remediation Checklist

With the increasing emphasis on reaching every student, so comes the question, "What have you done to specifically help each student achieve?" Yet with budget cuts necessitating larger class sizes, it can sometimes be difficult to remember what you did for each student. This kind of checklist, which could be included in a grade book or saved to your workstation, serves a dual purpose, though: it also functions as documentation of intervention strategies.

Student's name _____ **Period** _____ **Class** _____

1st quarter grade	**2nd quarter grade**	**3rd quarter grade**	**4th quarter grade**
_____	_____	_____	_____

Strategies attempted

❏ Established a personal connection

❏ Met with student

❏ Reviewed student's history

❏ Called or e-mailed parents

❏ Requested parent conference

❏ Referred to child study

❏ Discussed situation with administrator

❏ Tutored student or worked one-on-one

❏ Enlisted the help of student or peer tutors

❏ Paired student with a study buddy

❏ Tailored curriculum to student interest when possible

❏ Spoke with student's counselor or coach

❏ Managed student choice, giving options when possible

❏ Differentiated instruction

❏ Used a variety of assessments

❏ Asked a reading teacher to assess student's reading ability

❏ Helped student set goals

❏ Used written behavior or learning contracts

Additional comments _____

_____

_____

_____

Communication

Date	Time	Phone number (H/W) or contact information	Result and comments

RESOURCE 25
Tutoring Schedule

Create tutoring or review sessions that target specific objectives, strands, or areas for improvement. Ask every teacher to participate in such a program because all are responsible for helping students succeed.

SOL Review Sessions for 2004

Session	Date	Teachers	Subject
1	February 2	Nancy Bellings & Jesse Holmes	**Multiple-Choice Tests:** scoring rules, test dissection, strategies and skills
2	February 9	Larry Smith & Alison Brown	**Main Ideas/Supporting Details:** topic sentences, details, paragraphing
3	February 23	Sue Stanton & Sarah Kincaid	**Introductions/Thesis Statements/Conclusions:** strategies, components
4	March 1	Chris Klein & Catherine Bowman	**Locating and Using Information:** working from outlines, discerning between two drafts
5	March 8	Marie Devry & Ellen Marinakis	**Usage/Mechanics:** grammar, punctuation, revision in multiple-choice and writing sections
March 9 and 10		*SOL Writing Exam*	
6	March 15	Danielle Washington & Donna Highlander	**Vocabulary:** prefixes, roots, suffixes, context clues, and other strategies
7	March 22	Michelle Lansing & John Gabriel	**Poetry/Literary Terms:** practice and sample questions
8	March 29	Latisha Jones & Debbie Stein	**More Poetry/Literary Terms:** more practice and sample questions
9	April 12	Jorge Ramos & Gary Shaw	**Research:** formatting, appropriate sources, documentation
10	April 19	Peter Grafton & Dara Klowski	**Reading:** strategies, concentrated practice with reading passages
11	April 26	Bill Schmidt & Laura Howe	**Consumer Literacy:** reading and filling out forms, applications, and warranties
12	May 3	Megan Yardley & Pam Jones	**Extra Practice:** practice with different multiple-choice passages
Date TBA		*SOL Reading, Literature, Research Exam*	**SUCCESS!**

- We may be able to hold one more session, on May 10, depending on the May SOL testing schedule. More on that to follow.

- In each of the sessions, students should be given a chance to work with multiple-choice practice questions.

- Materials will be provided to aid teacher teams in planning and teaching their sessions. These materials should guide teachers in planning their sessions and should be complemented with any additional materials the teacher teams wish to use.

- Emphasis should be on skill building and test practice.

RESOURCE 26
Class Evaluation Survey

Just as teachers want to have a voice in how their school is run, students feel the same about their classes. Some teachers are afraid to seek student input and feedback because they fear relinquishing control, but holding class meetings with each period is one way to foster and build community. Giving students a voice can oftentimes improve motivation, morale, and climate.

Administer a survey that students fill out anonymously a few times during the year to assess how they feel about their progress, the class, and the like; then follow up with them by sharing and discussing the results. You might prefer using a Likert scale instead of short response questions, but either format will yield important information.

1. How has the pace of instruction been so far?

2. Can you list three essential items that you have learned?

3. What type of instruction has appealed to you the most (group work, independent work, class discussion, overhead instruction, PowerPoint presentations, etc.) and why?

4. Have I been approachable and responsive to your needs? Why or why not?

5. Have I been available when you needed me?

6. Do you think that you need extra help? If so, what kind? In which areas?

7. Are you happy with your present grade?

8. If not, what three things do you plan to do to improve it?

9. Do you have a favorite class session? A least favorite class session?

10. What do you enjoy most about class? Least about class?

11. How confident do you feel in your ability to succeed in this class?

12. Do you believe that your grades have been fair and lacking bias?

13. Do you think that your study skills have improved this year? If so, in what areas? Where do you still need to improve?

14. What from the first semester/quarter are you most proud of?

15. What from the first semester/quarter are you least proud of?

16. What goals do you have for this new quarter/semester? What steps will you take to achieve them?

17. If you achieved your first semester goals, how did you do so?

18. What advice, suggestions, and words of wisdom would you give to future students taking this class?

19. What suggestions do you have to improve class?

20. General comments?

RESOURCE 27
Reading Accountability Sheet

Sustained Silent Reading (SSR) can be an important way to improve a student's reading ability. Talk to your teachers about including SSR in their classes because all disciplines can find a way to incorporate this strategy. For example, a government class could read Newsweek, a physical education class could read a biography of an athlete, and so on.

There is no foolproof system to keep track of students' reading, but below is one way to try to ensure that students are sticking with the same book. You might also have students write a brief synopsis of what they read so that they demonstrate understanding and, on some level, interact with what they read. Future students could review these synopses to see if they might be interested in the book.

Name _____   Period _____   SSR Week # _____

Please record your book title and page number daily. This log will be collected weekly.

Monday	Tuesday	Wednesday	Thursday	Friday
Date:	Date:	Date:	Date:	Date:
Title:	Title:	Title:	Title:	Title:
Pages:	Pages:	Pages:	Pages:	Pages:
What happened in today's reading?	What happened in today's reading?	What happened in today's reading?	What happened in today's reading?	What happened in today's reading?

RESOURCE 28
Test Prep Tip Sheet

Some teachers bristle at the suggestion of teaching test-taking strategies, but test prep does not always have to be about finding shortcuts. It is a way to make students savvy test-takers who will know what to expect and what they should do. If your teachers don't conduct any kind of test preparation, then they are sending their students onto the battlefield without arming them as best as possible.

1. *Practice.* Practice tests can help teachers and students identify areas for improvement. Let students take full-length versions of released tests or tests similar to the one they will need to take. A month before the test, students might complete sample problems as warm-ups. Discuss correct answers, or pair students together and have them write explanations for correct (or incorrect) answers.

2. *Know the format.* Students also should take practice tests because they need to be exposed to the format of the test—how it is structured, how questions and answers are organized, and so on. You might even set up your own tests and midterms to resemble the format of the high-stakes test. In addition, you should explain how the test is scored (whether points are taken off for skipped questions, what is considered passing, etc.).

3. *Read the directions carefully.* Although this might seem obvious, some students ignore directions, gloss over them, or don't fully listen while they are being read. Break your students of this habit.

4. *Reread the question.* Students should be trained to read the question carefully and even to mark it up. If students are stuck after reading all answer choices, they should go back to the question because there is a good chance that they misread it. Many students will simply continue reading answer choices instead of going back to the question itself.

5. *Write on the test.* Students should be active test-takers: they should always have a pencil in hand so that they can underline key phrases in a question, cross out answers, and make notes on a reading passage, chart, or graph. Instruct students to look for key words or terms.

6. *Anticipate answers.* Train students to anticipate the answer to a question, to compare their gut answer to the answer choices, and to eliminate incongruous choices. During practice, you might even encourage students to cover up the answers while they read the question.

7. *Eliminate similar or synonymous answers.* Show students the value of narrowing down their answer choices. If there are three very similar answers dealing with aerobic respiration and only one that deals with anaerobic respiration, students can sometimes make an educated guess that the single answer is the correct choice.

8. *Be completely right.* As with a true/false question, if any part of the answer is incorrect, then the answer choice must be crossed off. Some students struggle here and pick the incorrect answer because they recognize a piece of correct information in the answer choice.

9. *Look for "turn words."* Show students how to pay careful attention to the wording of a question, because words and phrases such as "except," "not," "least," and "all of the following" can signal that the correct answer will be antithetical to what is stated in the beginning of the question.

10. *Skip questions.* Students should skip questions if they are stuck and return to them later with a clearer mind and a fresh outlook. A faint mark in the margin can help remind them of where to come back to. But show students how these marks, or any stray ones, can be picked up by the scanner as a response, which can cause the answer to be wrong.

11. *Apply proper bubbling.* This is important because if a student skips one question but continues to bubble in the normal answer slots, every answer could potentially be wrong. Similarly, students need to know where to bubble in answers to sample questions; sometimes students record them into actual answer slots, thereby throwing off the scoring of their entire test.

12. *Silently read aloud.* For some students, high-stakes tests are as much stamina tests as they are tests of knowledge. Encourage students to silently mouth out what they read, especially for reading passages. This can help them concentrate and focus, because their minds are less likely to wander when they do this.

RESOURCE 29
Data Tracker

Tracking student progress will become even more important over the next few years as a result of No Child Left Behind. Creating a system to chart areas for improvement can help facilitate achievement. After each test or assessment, a teacher can determine where a student needs to improve as well as compare a student's progress or growth to previous assessments or to the class as a whole. This example uses strands from the SAT verbal section, but it can easily be adapted to use state learning objectives. Similarly, if your teachers don't already use electronic grade book programs, they can create a spreadsheet to help students track their grades.

Student	Date	Score	Analogy questions missed			Sentence completion questions missed			Reading comprehension questions missed				
			Easy	Medium	Difficult	Easy	Medium	Difficult	Main Idea	Vocab in Context	Para-phrase	Infer-ence	Paired Passages

RESOURCE 30
Interview on Using Data

Below is the complete transcript from the interview with Paul Farmer, the principal of Kilmer Middle School in Fairfax County, Virginia, that is summarized in Chapter 6. Farmer offers specific advice for working with data and outlines his expectations for teacher leaders regarding data.

John Gabriel: First, the term "teacher leader" can encompass such a large range of responsibilities, so whom exactly are you referring to or who receives and analyzes data in your building?

Paul Farmer: By teacher leader, I'm referring to team leaders and department chairs—those leaders who are directly responsible for leading and supervising teachers in a department or on a team. My chairs receive data in the form of grade reports and SOL results [Standards of Learning, the high-stakes test in Virginia] from their administrators, but if they don't, they need to ask for them because they are such an important part of instructional leadership and of improving an instructional program.

JG: When you talk of improving an instructional program, I assume that one of the things you're referring to is "data-driven instruction." How do you interpret that phrase, or more specifically, how do you ask your chairs to interpret that phrase?

PF: Data-driven instruction is the use of student data and analysis of these data to make instructional decisions to change or maintain the habit of instruction or the current instructional methods. The data are either going to say that "yes, this is good," or that something needs to be addressed.

JG: So teachers shouldn't be married to a particular methodology because it is fashionable or because they like it?

PF: Exactly. Data are one way of determining what works and what doesn't work.

JG: What are your expectations of teacher leaders when they receive data?

PF: I expect a teacher leader to know his data and work with the results with his department or team. I expect him to come to me and say, "This is what I determined needs to happen and here are the resources I need to make that happen." I expect him to understand the data, know the data, and be comfortable with the data and how to use the data.

JG: But not all chairs have this kind of understanding. What do you do for them?

PF: I conduct in-house training where I make them aware of the available programs that break down the standardized test data by gender, race, and the like. I also show them how to interpret classroom data in terms of interim, marking period, and semester averages, and I expect them to then explain these things to their teachers. But I have brought in outside resources to train not just my teacher leaders but my administrative team as well because they too will be working closely with a chair and his data.

JG: After a chair receives his data, what next?

PF: Obviously, I expect him to digest the information and reflect on it, possibly even try to draw conclusions from it. Then he shares the departmental data as a whole with his department. He can share his thoughts, ask for others' insight, and so on at this time. It's a good way for teams to discuss what is or isn't going on in the classroom or obstacles they are facing. The teachers will get their own data in comparison to the department's and draw their own conclusions too. The chair will display a graph on the overhead showing a teacher's number next to GPA. But each teacher will receive a handout that has his name in place of one of the numbers so that he can see where he stands in relation to the department.

I want my chairs to do the same with standardized test data. The graphs start with the highest grade average or the highest passing rate and proceed to the lowest. Again, the desired outcome is that this opens up discussion so it's not me or the department chair saying, "You have to do this" or "This is what you need to do." Instead, it is the teachers saying, "Here's I what I think I need to do. What do you think?" And teachers receiving data generally fall into one of two categories. One group is comprised of teachers who have a higher average of results in a particular strand [in terms of data yielded by high-stakes tests] and the other is comprised of teachers who have a lower average in a particular strand. This helps teachers in the department grow [and learn from one another].

JG: How else do you have your teacher leaders working with data?

PF: SOL data, class grades and averages, comparisons of those averages to SOL scores—I want my leaders to see if these sets of data are running parallel. For example, if a teacher has a high number of *A*s, I want my chairs to see if this correlates to SOL results being in the advanced range.

JG: And this covers the inverse as well?

PF: It would. We discuss that. So by the same token, if a teacher has a high number of *D*s or *F*s, I expect that teacher to have a high number of students scoring only in the proficient range or not passing the test. When there is a discrepancy [students performing poorly in class but well on high-stakes tests, and vice versa], it can indicate that there is a problem in the class. It can also give a chair, or even the teacher, important information about what is, or is not, occurring in the class, what a teacher is really assessing or teaching. And it can also say that students are getting damaged. Students see that they are working really hard but aren't achieving by the teacher's measure, although they are by the state's measure. That can really turn off a student's drive and desire for education.

JG: But do these data show that you have an effective or ineffective teacher?

PF: The data do not determine if the teacher is a good teacher or not. Data might indicate that change is needed, but more important, such factual information allows you to start a dialogue. Without data, the dialogue is based on opinions and observations, and some might even claim ambitions. Without the data, how do you identify the goal? Moreover, how do you measure the change or the growth?

JG: How do your teachers feel about receiving this kind of information?

PF: Your more confident teachers are open to it and embrace it. They're looking for more, want it broken down in different ways and in as many ways as possible—by period, by race, and even by zip code when possible. As a norm, their grades aren't always strong, but they crave more information to make decisions and base adjustments on.

JG: And how do the other teachers react when presented with this information?

PF: Well, on the other end of the spectrum are the teachers who look at the data and say, "So what?" or "So what does this mean?" or "Are you trying to tell me that I'm a bad teacher?" Or they're looking for me or their chair to tell them what the problem is. These teachers take a little more work because I don't pull these data or ask my chairs to use these data to be critical. Rather, it's about giving these teachers information that is specific to them so that they can attempt to make decisions dealing with instructional change. And again, in speaking of norms, these teachers tend to be a little less confident and seem to feel that people are trying to tell them what they're doing is wrong instead of seeing the process as a way to help them grow.

JG: How can a teacher leader help accomplish this?

PF: The teacher leader has got to believe that he has backbone or support, confident that his administrator is going to back him in hard changes. If he isn't confident of that administrative support, he ceases to be a teacher leader and becomes passive—and that is not the fault of the chair but of the administrator. I demonstrate open communication with the teacher leader and show that he is supported, is trusted as the instructional leader and curricular expert, and is seen as an advisor. And I expect this kind of rapport and trust to be mutual. An effective instructional leader doesn't have the administrative power to make change, so he must have administrative support if a recommendation for change is made.

JG: When you say that you see your teacher leaders as advisors, do you look to them to make recommendations based on the data they have analyzed?

PF: Definitely.

JG: So after a chair has addressed his department, he needs to speak with his individual teachers. How does he proceed with a teacher who has a high ratio of *D*s and *F*s?

PF: The first thing I suggest is for my teacher leaders to ask their teachers after they have seen the data, "What does this mean to you?" or "What do you make of this?" They need to ask those leading questions to see if the teacher will go into the "analyze-and-adjust mode." The very next question a teacher leader needs to ask is "What can I do for you that would be helpful?"

JG: So your hope is that your chair is able to get his teachers to reflect on their practices based on data or to understand that a change might be needed. What if that doesn't happen?

PF: As I said, the chair needs to see how willing teachers are to reflect and consider alternative practices. If they are not initially receptive to this, I like to see my chairs offer their teachers some time to think about what was shared. Then the teacher leaders need to ask their teachers to come up with suggestions or solutions that might improve the situation. And the chair needs to keep his administrator apprised of what has been taking place.

JG: What exactly should he be informing his administrator about?

PF: The teacher is either going to answer in one of two ways: I don't have any ideas, or let me think about it. In the meantime, a chair and his administrator need to have a dialogue about what directions they feel the teacher should be moving. Again, I'm expecting the chair to give me some guidance on what is needed to improve the situation.

JG: So what happens when the teacher tells his chair that he "just can't think of any solutions"?

PF: I would ask my chair if he is comfortable enough to give a directive or if he would rather have administrative intervention.

JG: But chairs can't really give directives, so how does that work?

PF: It works because the chair is acting as an agent of the administration. If I'm confident in my chair, in his knowledge of instruction and curriculum, then he can tell the teacher that he's making the same suggestion to the administration regarding the situation—and expects to be supported. And if the teacher decides to go and complain to the administration, she will discover that we support the chair and have the same recommendation for her. After this happens with one or two teachers, the word gets around and the message gets across, so you have chairs making de facto directives.

JG: And what if a quarter or a semester later the data still indicate the same things?

PF: Assuming there aren't any extenuating circumstances, if nothing improves, then the teacher is not attempting to change. Personally, I'd rather see a teacher take risks and maybe even not succeed because that means she is at least open to change. So the next step, of course, is that the administrator needs to counsel with the teacher, and depending on the administrator's preference, with or without the chair, review the data again, and again determine what the teacher plans to do differently.

JG: Even if the administrator asks his chair to be present, doesn't the teacher have the right to ask that he not be there?

PF: Yes, but the administrator should do everything he can to counsel the teacher toward wanting the chair there for support.

JG: Why is that?

PF: Because it's the administrator's job to be the hammer, so when possible, I would want my chair to be seen as a support.

JG: And what if the teacher is defiant when your chair speaks with him?

PF: My chair's job is not to come down on someone. Dialogue between the chair and his administrator is essential. If defiance sets in on the teacher's part, there has to be clear communication from the administrator that such behavior is not acceptable and what is in place is not acceptable. At some point, I'm the one who needs to request, if not require, change—positive change.

JG: Is there anything else you expect your teacher leader to do with data?

PF: I like to see my chairs sharing data with other schools with comparable populations, to see what else can be learned through collaboration. I like to see chairs grow by using the data to support their own ambitions and professional growth. Basically, I want my chair to be a role model for using data to reflect on their own population.

Index

About the Author

John Gabriel has taught in three different school systems as an English teacher; after six years of teaching, he was hired as the English department chair at Falls Church High School in Fairfax County, Virginia. After two years of his dynamic and creative leadership, the English department achieved such dramatic gains on high-stakes tests that it soared to parity with departments at high-achieving schools in the area. He received his bachelor's degree from Mary Washington College, graduating with honors in English and in education. He also holds a master's degree in educational leadership from George Mason University and is a member of Phi Delta Kappa. Gabriel has led staff development sessions and retreats for instructional leaders; he has conducted workshops on assessments, effecting change in schools, organizational strategies, differentiation, and vocabulary development. Now an administrator at Park View High School in Loudoun County, Virginia, he can be reached at gabrielresearch@msn.com.

Related ASCD Resources: Teacher Leadership

At the time of publication, the following ASCD resources were available; for the most up-to-date information about ASCD resources, go to www.ascd.org. ASCD stock numbers are noted in parentheses.

Audio

Balanced Leadership: What Research Shows About Leadership and Student Achievement by Tim Waters, Robert J. Marzano, and Brian McNulty (2 Audiotapes #204169; 2 CDs #504303)

Building Internal Capacity: Identifying and Developing Teacher Leaders by Michaelene Meyer (Audiotape #202216)

Developing Leadership Skills Through Dialogue by Laura Billings and Terry Roberts (Audiotape #204186; CD #504320)

Teacher Leaders: Who Are They? Why Do We Need Them? by Thomas Gannon (Audiotape #204183; CD #504317)

Networks

Visit the ASCD Web site (www.ascd.org) and click on About ASCD. Go to the section on Networks for information about professional educators who have formed groups around topics such as "Instructional Supervision," "Mentoring Leadership and Resources," "Performance Assessment for Leadership," and "Women's Leadership Issues." Look in the Network Directory for current facilitators' addresses and phone numbers.

Online Courses

Visit the ASCD Web site (www.ascd.org) for the following professional development opportunities:

Contemporary School Leadership by Vera Blake (#PD04OC38)

Effective Leadership by Frank Betts (#PD98OC04)

Print Products

Educational Leadership, April 2004: Leading in Tough Times (entire issue #104029)

Finding Your Leadership Style: A Guide for Educators by Jeffrey Glanz (#102115)

Guide for Instructional Leaders, Guide 1: An ASCD Action Tool by Roland Barth, Bobb Darnell, Laura Lipton, and Bruce Wellman (#702110)

Leadership Capacity for Lasting School Improvement by Linda Lambert (#102283)

Lessons from Exceptional School Leaders by Mark Goldberg (#101229)

On Becoming a School Leader: A Person-Centered Challenge by Arthur W. Combs, Ann B. Miser, and Kathryn S. Whitaker (#199024)

Video

The Teacher Series Tapes 4–6: *Teacher as Peer Coach, Teacher as Staff Developer, Teacher as Reflective Learner* (3 Videotapes and Facilitator's Guide #401089)

For more information, visit us on the World Wide Web (www.ascd.org), send an e-mail message to member@ascd.org, call the ASCD Service Center (1-800-933-ASCD or 703-578-9600, then press 2), send a fax to 703-575-5400, or write to Information Services, ASCD, 1703 N. Beauregard St., Alexandria, VA 22311-1714 USA.

DATE DUE